TUNISIA

A Personal View of a Timeless Land

TUNISIA

A Personal View of a Timeless Land

JOHN ANTHONY

NEW YORK

CHARLES SCRIBNER'S SONS

LINE DRAWINGS BY THE AUTHOR

PICTURE CREDITS

BLACK STAR: opposite pages 70, 134
PAUL POPPER LTD.: opposite pages 34, 142, 148, 172, 188, 192
TUNISIAN OFFICE OF TOURISM: opposite pages 50, 164
TUNISIAN TRADE AND TOURIST OFFICE, NEW YORK: opposite pages
20, 28, 44, 98, 130, 188, 206

FOR

SUE

ACKNOWLEDGMENTS

The historical sections of this book are based for the most part on such standard works as Plutarch, Gibbon and the Cambridge Histories. For my account of Moslem history and religion I have also used Alfred Guillaume: *Islam* (Penguin Books, 1954); the *Shorter Encyclopedia of Islam* edited by J. H. Kramers, H. A. R. Gibb and E. Levi-Provençal (E. J. Brill, Leiden, 1953); and the *Atlas of Islamic History* compiled by Harry W. Hazard (Princeton University Press, 1952). Much information concerning historical places and monuments comes from *Les Guides Bleus: Algérie-Tunisie* (Hachette, Paris, 1950). I have also consulted *Tunisie: Atlas historique, géographique, économique et touristique* (Horizons de France, Paris, 1936) and Paul Sebag: *La Tunisie: essaie de monographie* (Editions Sociales, Paris, 1951). The account of the martyrs of Carthage is taken from Omer Englebert: *The Lives of the Saints,* translated by Christopher and Anne Fremantle (Thames and Hudson, 1951). *The Prolegomena of ibn Khaldoun* has been translated by Franz Rosenthal under the title of *The Muqaddimah: an Introduction to History* (Routledge and Kegan Paul, 1958).

The quotations from the Koran are my own adaptations of translations by Mohammed Marmaduke Pickthall (*The Meaning of the Glorious Koran,* G. Allen, 1930) and Abdullah Yusuf Ali (*The Holy Qur-an,* Copyright. Khalil al-Rawaf. Cambridge, Mass., 1946). The quotation from Cicero is by Edith Hamilton (*The Roman Way,* Dent, 1933); that from St. Augustine by

7

Acknowledgments

Edward E. Pusey (*The Confessions of St. Augustine,* Dent (Everyman's Library), 1933); those from Herodotus by Aubrey de Selincourt (Herodotus: *The Histories,* Penguin Books, 1954); and that from Homer by E. V. Rieu (*The Odyssey,* Methuen, 1946). The remark made by Ronald Firbank about the beauty of Sfax is quoted by Sacheverel Sitwell in *Mauretania: Warrior, Man and Woman* (Duckworth, 1940). I wish I could find the name of the modern poet who said that olive trees wear 'the hue of distance'.

Not being handy with a camera, my thanks are due to the following for allowing me to use photographs: Paul Popper Ltd., Black Star and The Tunisian Office of Tourism.

J. A.

CONTENTS

ILLUSTRATIONS

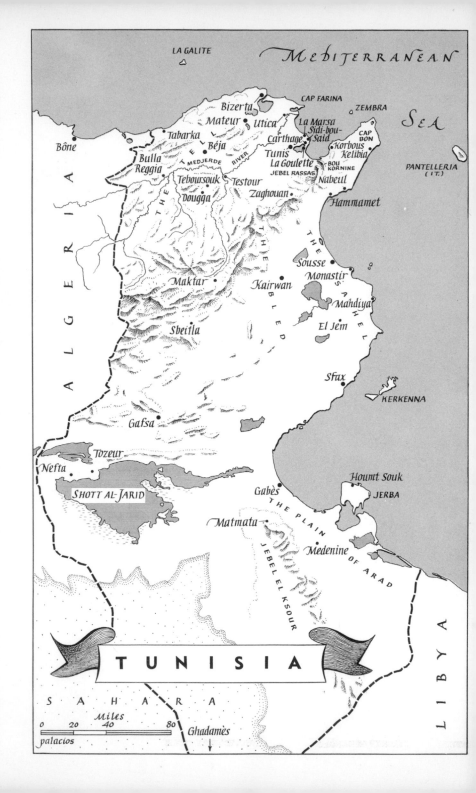

LA GALITE

MEDITERRANEAN

CAP FARINA

ZEMBRA

SEA

Bizerta
Mateur
Utica
La Marsa
Sidi-bou-
Said
CAP
BON
Tabarka
Carthage
Korbous
Kelibia

Bône
Béja
Tunis
BOU
KORNINE
La Goulette
JEBEL RASSAS
Nabeul
Bulla
Reggia
Teboursouk
Testour
Zaghouan
Hammamet

A L G E R I A

T H E   T E L L

MEDJERDE   RIVER

Dougga

PANTELLERIA
(IT.)

Maktar

Kairwan

Sousse
Monastir
Mahdiya

T H E   K R O U M I R I E

El Jem

Sbeitla

T H E   S A H E L

Sfax

KERKENNA

Gafsa

Tozeur

Nefta

SHOTT AL-JARID

Houmt Souk
JERBA

Gabès

Matmata

THE PLAIN OF ARAD

Medenine

JEBEL EL KSOUR

T U N I S I A

L I B Y A

S A H A R A

Miles
0   20   40   80

palacios

Ghadamès

INTRODUCTION

WHEN I FIRST WENT TO TUNISIA IN THE LAST DAYS OF THE FRENCH Protectorate, I was a bachelor. When I left five years later, Tunisia had gained her independence and I had lost mine. The facts are disproportionate, but this is a personal, not a political account, in which private affairs play a larger part than public ones. Although I was in Tunisia for my government, I have not written a book about politics or diplomacy. This is an account of life in Tunisia, of scenes and events that affected me, of friends and memorable acquaintances, of travels, reading, and vagrant thoughts. It is above all an effort to understand another way, or ways, of life, to find the values other people place on the elements of their existence, and thereby find a touchstone for our own. If we return from a voyage without a feeling that our own ways are a little peculiar, we might as well stay home.

"Ways of life": the plural is necessary. Tunisia is a country of astonishing contrasts and variety. Set almost in the centre of the Mediterranean, she has been involved in most of the currents and conflicts of that turbulent basin. Her northern harbours gape toward the underbelly of Europe; her long eastern shore faces across Libya to Egypt and the Levant; her western hills merge into the great Atlas landmass that runs to the Atlantic; her southern roots trail off into the Sahara toward the heart of Africa. She has been Berber, Phoenician, Roman, Vandal, Byzantine, Arab, Turkish, and French—her people

13

pagan, Christian, Jewish, and Moslem. Old and important events took place here, and contributions to many civilisations sprang from this soil. The young and energetic Republic of Tunisia draws its *élan* from many sources.

In an effort to comprehend this variety, I have hung my book on a frame of geography, starting in the north and environs of Tunis where I lived, moving westward, then into central Tunisia, and ending with a tour of the south. This method violates chronology, both personal and historical, but it emphasises the spirit of place, which is more important and, in Tunisia especially, exercises a powerful spell.

If I were to choose a single image to represent Tunisia—like those figures of popular iconography, John Bull, Uncle Sam, or Marianne—I would choose one of the veiled women of Tunis. Morocco is a land of harsh, castellated mountains guarded by a race of warriors. Algeria is a no-nonsense country of farms, mines, and banks; your average Algerian is a business-man or farmer who can become a guerilla when pressed. Tunisia by contrast is feminine: the landscape horizontal with gradual transitions and soft, swelling shores, the climate mild and slightly enervating, the blue-green sea, the pervasive scent of jasmine and orange blossoms, the husky plaintive voice of an Andalusian song. The temperament of the people is gay, evanescent, tender—not fierce like that of Moroccans, nor stolid like Algerians. Tunisians have what the Arabs call 'light blood' and the French have termed '*la douceur arabe*.' But Tunisia can also be dangerous: magic and witchcraft are prevalent, precautions must be taken against the evil eye, murders are committed for enigmatic reasons of jealousy, honour, or revenge.

Above all Tunisia preserves an air of mystery. Perhaps this stems from the Arab passion for privacy: the veiled women, the blank walls and barred and latticed windows, the impenetrable family life, the mosques forbidden to the infidel. The woman of Tunis I have chosen to represent Tunisia wears a white silk *ha'ik* enveloping her figure; her face is hidden by a black mask; only the eyes are visible, dark and luminous in a rim of *kohl*. This is a romantic image, but Tunisia is still a romantic country. The veil implies an infinity of possibilities. Is she young or old, dark or fair, smiling or disdainful—a nymph or a witch? Let us lift the veil.

I. TUNIS

"ALL CITIES ARE FOUNDED ON FEAR," SAID THE WHITE FATHER. "You can see what Tunis was afraid of—" he waved a hand toward the open sea.

I had come up on deck to watch our arrival and had found the old priest standing almost exactly where I had left him the night before. It was a precarious, early spring day, fair and foul by turns; right now it had settled to a thin, cold rain, almost erasing the coastline that lay dim as a mirage on the horizon. Not what I had expected of my first glimpse of Africa. My companion was ambiguous too. From behind, he looked like an Arab: a white wool *burnous* hung in a stiff pyramid from his shoulders; his head was covered with a cherry red *chechia*, a black silk tassel dangling down his back. But in front, a gold crucifix gleamed among the folds, and there was no mistaking that face—broad, pink, and northern, probably Flemish. He was an enormous man, tall and broad-shouldered, and spoke in booming peasant French with an occasional Arabic word or phrase that seemed to come more quickly to his tongue. He was returning from some errand in France to Barbary, as he called it, his home for the past twenty years.

"Tunis knew what to expect from the sea," he said, "being a pirate power herself. Practically everyone has invaded Barbary at some time. Even you British and Americans did it a few years ago."

A low cape stretched ahead of us like a restraining arm, its shoulder hunched up in the shape of a volcano. "Cap Bon," said the priest, "'Tunis' first line of defence. An enemy could be sighted from its tip and the alarm relayed by fast boat or fire beacons to the city. And those two islands—Zembra and Zembretta—were used to ambush an attacker. Handy for pirates and smugglers too."

Our ship veered southward into the shelter of Cap Bon and into a wide-mouthed harbour. On our right, a red cliff rode into view with a white village on its back. "In ancient times," the White Father said with a touch of pride, "Carthage was not afraid to stand on the open sea. That village is a suburb of the old city, now called Sidi-bou-Saïd. And that next hill is Byrsa, Dido's mountain. Thunes was just a miserable village then."

Dido's mountain looked low and rather suburban, with a twin-towered church unexpectedly on top and a smudge of buildings on the slopes. We were nearer land now, and the coastline rolled past like an old-fashioned film, fuzzy and grey with rain. Buildings and roads grew thicker on the shore, and the water began to quicken with a traffic of small boats. We were heading for some docks, which I guessed were Tunis.

"Not at all," said my companion. "Tunis is more prudent. This is La Goulette, literally 'a throat' which we shall pass through presently into the lake. La Goulette was another outwork of the city, which could be closed with chains and covered by cannon from the fort."

Under the frowning battlements, a harbour full of yachts and fishing boats and a ribbon of beach with cafés and bathing huts looked bedraggled in the rain. We sailed up to the town into what seemed the mouth of a river on whose banks lay an angular landscape of cranes, jetties, and sheds. But it was a two-dimensional town, and in a few minutes we had passed through it and into the lake of Tunis.

"We are in the channel dredged by the French," the priest

said. "The lake is shallow and muddy-bottomed, with marshes and lagoons along the shore to bog down an invader who got this far. That little island with the ruined fortress was the last defence of Tunis, before you got to the mud flats and the walls. And here" (there was a long interval between each of my companion's statements, as the ship progressed toward the port) "here is your Tunis at last."

The city lay at the foot of the lake, like a paranoid pasha cowering behind ring after ring of locked and guarded walls. The modern town was hidden by a bristling screen of piers and warehouses. Behind it, the Arab city rose in a series of terraces, composed like a cubist painting of straight lines and flat white planes, washed by the rain to a dull pewter glow. I began to feel the excitement of approaching land and thought of Aeneas and those first Phoenician adventurers who must have landed somewhere on this very shore.

On the dock, descendants of pirates in blue overalls and bandanna turbans waited to board us. The White Father shouted a farewell and, clutching his one small bag, was first down the gangplank. A pirate scrambled past him and, muttering "*douane—gomrick*—customs", seized my things. I plunged behind him into the maelstrom of the port, guarded by the hydra-jaws of the law. "Birth place of father? maiden name of mother? length of sojourn? . . . dollars? Swiss francs? travellers' cheques? letter of credit? . . . address? hotel? friends? . . . cigarettes? drugs? watches? camera?" A couple of hours later I was in a battered but game pre-War Renault headed for a hotel.

Tunis was like a slap in the face. I have become reconciled to finding places like Paris, Rome, or even Athens having an independent life of their own and behaving as if they were the centre of the world. But Tunis, a town one had scarcely heard of, should know its place. It ought to wear a somnolent, peripheral air, waiting to be discovered by the adventurous traveller. Nothing of the sort. The wet streets were congested with shouting, gesticulating people, all apparently bent on errands of life or death. It was not a crowd: everyone remained an individual, separate and fiercely competitive, treating everyone else as an obstacle to be shoved aside or got around. We slid along the dangerously slick streets while other cars shot by us and pedestrians dashed in front. My driver manœuvred the high-slung Renault with hair-raising skill and swore venomously at passers-by in several languages. As he swiped a place in front of the hotel, I noticed that the taxi-meter had not been turned on.

"Pay whatever you like," he smiled villainously. I knew this trick: perhaps I would offer too much; if not, there would be a scene.

"Wait till I've changed some money," I said and went into the hotel. I asked the registration clerk to pay the correct fare and put it on my bill.

My room was glacial, the heating regulated by the calendar, not the thermometer. I thought: give me a cold country in winter, a hot one in summer; each copes best with its own speciality. Without unpacking, I went for a walk.

The streets were even more intimidating on foot. I was quickly pushed off the pavement and into the gutter, where taxis sped recklessly by and iron-wheeled carriages cracked warning whips over my head. Café tables were spread across the sidewalks, and the gutters themselves were clogged with little knots of angry debaters. Other pedestrians eddied round them or pushed through, but, not so brave as the others, I darted through a break in traffic to a tree-lined promenade down the centre of the boulevard. Immediately I was beset by a band of ragged boys, brandishing the stumps of arms or legs: "Mines, American grenades, mutilated by the War," they called gaily, and offered me shoelaces, chewing gum, or unspecified services in the Old City. I hurried on between

A Tunisian cafe

ranks of flower sellers, newspaper kiosks, and vendors of lottery tickets.

Tunis la verte: "White Algiers and green Tunis" one reads in Arab poetry and French travel folders. But Tunis was the colour of putty. Everything was covered with a thin skin of mud; in dry weather, I learned, this would be a dust that sifted into eyes and nostrils, and the cracks of drawers. I also noted a peculiar smell, at first I thought the usual Mediterranean mixture of roasting coffee and fresh urine; but there was something else, sulphurous and vaguely sinister. It was a smell I was to become familiar with and to identify as the stagnant water of the lake.

I came to the end of the boulevard and debouched on to a square that seemed to be the eye of the human whirlpool. In the centre some tall, ragged palm trees flanked a war memorial; the façade of a cathedral gazed blankly across from one end of the square to a heavily guarded public building at the other. Streams of people flowed in, around, and out of the square by some sort of diastolic action. The variety was startling. In most places there is a homogeneity about the inhabitants, a few themes of dress and physique to be grasped, with only an occasional surprise. Tunis was all surprises. There was no pattern, no norm from which to measure the variations of physiognomy or dress. The faces ranged from milk-white to ebony, with every shade of olive, copper, or coffee in between; the features set in them covered the gamut of human possibilities. Arab dress appeared to admit no limit of style or fashion: it included the flowing and the straight, the brilliant and the drab, the turban, the fez, the *chechia*, and the astrakhan; and many wore a mixture of native and western dress. Only the women, I thought, looked uniform, swathed from head to ankles in thin white sheets—but here came one wrapped in a bright striped blanket, and there was a group of girls, bare faced and bare footed, in dark blue *chitons*. Even the Europeans followed no standard: they wore the dress of their country of origin, and any traveller knows that Europe is not sartorially united. It was like Quattrocento Florence where, it is said, no fashion prevailed and everyone dressed as he pleased.

To the civilian masquerade was added an extraordinary motley of uniforms, religious and military. White Fathers, Capuchins, lay priests in black *soutanes* and white jabots swarmed in and out of the cathedral, and a confectioner's tray of starched and pleated nuns moved up and down its broad steps. In the cathedral door lurked a beadle in Second Empire scarlet and gold. Decorous serpentines of black-smocked school children threaded the crowd; and *chaouches*—braided and befrogged relics of the days of foreign capitulations—ran through on official errands. Across the square, the public building which was then the French Residency General was guarded by units of France's polychrome army—black Senegalese, tough little paratroopers fresh from Indo-China, Moroccan *goums*, the international ranks of the Foreign Legion, fresh-faced *matelots* and Tunisia's own musical comedy Beylical Guards.

Picturesque, but exhausting. Tired and dispirited I fought my way back to the hotel. The bar was empty at that hour. I surveyed the rows of sweet, weak apéritifs.

"Have you got any whisky?" I asked the bartender.

He had: an unknown brand at four hundred francs a shot. I ordered a double and wondered why I had ever come to Tunis.

Luckily I soon thought of Roxane. During the War a friend of mine had been stationed in Tunisia; when he heard I was going there he said immediately, "Then you must meet Roxane," the way one might say to a traveller to Rome, "You must have an audience with the Pope," or to Paris "Don't miss the Mona Lisa." For some reason—we are all poor draughtsmen—I had imagined someone terribly sleek, with a pale gold sheen and cool knowingness. Instead, when we arranged to meet, I found a woman who was all warmth and colour, the natural product of centuries of breeding and civilisation. Roxane's life touched almost every shore of the Mediterranean. Born in the Levant of one of those commercial dynasties of British, French, or Dutch origin, she had lived under Greek, then Turkish rule, and now possessed a French passport through marriage. She had lived for a time in Italy and frequently visited relations in England; during the War she had worked for the Americans. She spoke most of the languages of the inland sea, and French and English without accent but with a precise, old fashioned elegance learned from governesses. Her style of dress was Byzantine. A Venetian ancestress gave her the clue to her colouring, and she made up her face with a touch of Eastern elaboration that gave her the intense, enamelled look of an icon. She dressed in rich, stained-glass colours, in copies of Fath and Lanvin that she had run up by a little dressmaker she knew.

Roxane had one very sensible rule of life: do without necessities if you must, but insist on the luxuries. Her money was tied up in one of those tiresome new countries where she did not care to live. Tunis suited her: she had a small apartment on a modest street in the New City. But she did not live there. She lived in the world, the eternal debutante constantly exclaiming:

How beauteous mankind is!
O brave new world that hath such creatures in it!

She was a widow, and now she lived for her friends. I have never known anyone with so many, and so many different kinds. Everyone counted on her tolerance and sympathy and felt better when she was around, alone or in company. She believed in the civilised virtues and herself had the rare one of good manners in a naughty world. Roxane enjoyed life, and what she did not enjoy—rudeness, prejudice, gossip—she ignored and so embarrassed no one.

Roxane introduced me to her friends, and to people we met at the theatre, in restaurants, or at parties. Through her I met a French industrialist and his wife; he a man of many weighty interests, among them mines of lead and phosphates in the south; she with one consuming interest in a protocol ridden society—where she was seated at dinners—but when she gave a dinner herself, working for days beforehand with the cook on complicated 19th century dishes stuffed wherever possible with *foie gras* and cheerfully stuffing her guests themselves like Strasbourg geese. The young Maltese patriot painfully confined to his apartment, dying of consumption caught in damp cellars where he had operated a clandestine radio to the Allies during the German occupation of Tunisia. And the young men in cafés, authentic if slightly tarnished members of the Tunisian *jeunesse dorée,* wearing Charvet shirts and driving Alfa Romeos, a few of them in and out of jail for sharp dealings in foreign exchange. The Italian countess whose father, a clock maker, had hidden the last independent Bey of Tunis for a few weeks in 1881 from the invading French, and who herself had all the aristocratic earmarks of flat shoes, baggy tweeds, and a passion for fishing. The romantic couple, an American who had come to Tunisia in uniform during the War and had fallen in love with a bedouin girl, a singer and dancer, staggeringly beautiful with tribal tattoos on her forehead and chin, who, to everyone's surprise, had made a conspicuously happy and successful marriage. The voluptuous Jewess from a small southern town who, after a career of notable marriages that took in a French title and a Swiss millionaire, was now back in Tunis contentedly settled down with a hardworking newspaperman of similar origins to her own. And a third beauty, half Turkish and half French, married to an Arab official, who slowly withdrew behind a cloud of opium smoke until she disappeared entirely. And the ex-Prime Minister who covered himself in emeralds and drank whisky from a teacup to spare the feelings of his fellow Moslems. And many more.

We went to parties together. One was a costume ball given by the nephew of a perennial cabinet minister in the family palace in the Medina. This was an annual event of Tunisian social life, and each year the host, a rich young bachelor, set a different theme, perhaps as a change from the prevailing heterogeneity. This year the ball was Spanish. Roxane put a rose in her hair and went as Carmen, and I was vaguely Mexican to represent Iberia in the New World. The palace was at the foot of a dark *cul-de-sac*, and the low door gave no hint of the revelry within. The courtyard was lit with torches and just inside the door was a huge, ornate picture frame in which each guest or couple was photographed. Among the tableaux were several infantas and grandees out of Velasquez, a couple of Don Quixotes, and a *maja* or two (clothed) from Goya. A young Tunisian came dressed as a Spanish Moor with a couple of Christian heads in each hand, and the French Residency group was affronted by this token of Arab nationalism. On the other hand, a French Army officer wore a Falangist uniform and barked Fascist slogans; and the Spanish consul was affronted. Another guest got drunk and threw a tray of cream pastries at the dancers (someone said he had been a Gaullist, and his targets were all Pétainists), and was asked to leave. We danced to Latin music in the courtyard and at midnight sat down to a champagne supper.

Roxane and I left while the party was still in progress. The alley was dark and cold, with only a faint echo of music or a woman's high laugh coming from within. As we walked through a black shadow, I stepped on something that was soft and moved. A man grunted and stood up, and we heard the whimper of a child. We had disturbed a poor bedouin family in their sleep.

The Sea Gate still stands at the foot of the Old City, detached and aloof, like a triumphal arch celebrating some forgotten victory. The city walls were knocked down here, and the old city and the new permitted to meet and mingle in an intercultural slum teeming with activity and various forms of life, like the stretch of beach between tides. Here were the earliest European consulates and Christian churches, the Rue des Maltais, Greek restaurants and Spanish student cafés, dealers in Venetian antiques and fabricators of those unfading funeral decorations beloved of Sicilians, an 'oriental bazaar' run by a tribe of Hindus, and the kind of shops whose owners stand in the doorways hissing at tourists, "Please to come in please have cup of coffee." A few of the oldest European families, established here long before the French occupation, still keep town houses in the lofty apartments above the shops. Here the motor traffic is diverted to the left or right, swinging around the Old City in both directions, to meet under the Kasbah, or fortified high point of the town. Behind the Kasbah the ramparts look out, naked and almost intact, from a cliff above another lake of mud that protected careful Tunis from the rear.

In a quite literal sense, the Old City was built for men and not machines. The streets are too narrow, crooked, and uneven to admit motor-cars or even horse-drawn vehicles. Here there is no geometry: the streets and walls follow the natural curves and angles of age-old needs and desires, apparently eccentric but in fact as inevitable as a river bed. In some sections you feel you are not out of doors at all but in the corridors of a large, rambling house. The streets are no more than corridor-wide, and many of them are roofed over with masonry vaults or slatted boards. Sometimes the corridor becomes a flight of stairs, or widens into a room-like square with a fountain against one wall and a roof supported by green and red striped pillars. At the junction of some streets a huge nail-studded door is hung, rusting now on its hinges, designed to close the corridor off at night or against the dangers of other times. Perhaps it is this domestic atmosphere that changes the angry human molecules that swirl through the open spaces of the New City into well-mannered human beings, for architecture can impose a mood as potent as music. Once beyond the fringes of the Old City, the frenzy abates and the tempo modulates to the contemplative commerce of the souks and the quiet, almost empty alleys of the residential quarters.

In the souks the corridors are lined with cupboards—little open-faced stalls big enough to hold one or two men, and crammed with Moroccan leather, Damascus silk, stuffs from India, Swiss watches and German gadgets, Italian glass, factory products from England and France, and an assortment of everything Tunisia produces. The cloth souk flutters with squares and lengths of brilliant sleazy materials like flags at a regatta. The wool merchants sit in cosy caves insulated from heat and cold with stacks of folded *burnouses*, blankets, and rugs. In souk al-Attarine the air is faint with the scent of rose and orange-flower waters, the dust of henna and spices, and the sickly odours of crumbling, coloured soaps in the shape of fish or a woman's hand. Modern perfumes are displayed in litre bottles set in vitrines that look like rococo sedan chairs. Some souks are factories as well as shops. In a tunnel that pierces the ground floor of a whole block, the ubiquitous *chechias* that cover most male heads in Tunisia are knitted, combed, steamed, pressed, and dyed a deep raspberry red. In the leather souk, rows of cross-legged cobblers cut, hammer, and stitch the soft coloured hides into the heel-less *babouches* of North Africa, or sew tinsel and sequins on slippers for Tunisian brides. The metal-workers' souk rings with the torments of over-wrought brass and copper. In the gold souk, the vitrines are filled with machine-turned jewellery with hard faceted stones, but from the drawers in back you can draw out soft blossoms of rose diamonds, Venetian and Turkish wrought gold, and heavy bedouin silver. I had my wallet snatched once in the gold souk; I gave chase and caught the thief, a lad of about fourteen who gave me such an apologetic smile that I let him go. Nearby is a small square that used to be the slave market, where you can sit and drink a cup of Turkish coffee and dream of more delectable wares.

My favourite walks were in the residential quarters high in the Medina. The meandering streets and blank, noncommittal walls seemed as uninhabited as one of di Chirico's urban vistas, and just as suggestive of hidden, mysterious life. An unexpected glimpse into a courtyard or garden, because it is unintended, seems freighted with significance. A silent figure vanishes into a hidden door, bent (surely!) on no prosaic errand. An Arab town is built like a maze: there is the same baffling choice of turnings, the need to remember your way back, the feeling you are *solving* something, like a riddle. Many of the streets end in *culs-de-sac* and have the name of *impasse*—Impasse du Sabre, Impasse No. 6. What an appropriate address that would be—Impasse No. 6. Often you realise you are lost, and an irrational fear stirs the hair on your spine. I soon learned, however, to follow the ball of twine: by turning my steps downhill I always emerged from the labyrinth. But disappointed, having found neither Ariadne nor the Minotaur.

It was Roxane, of course, who first took me into one of those mysterious gardens behind the noncommittal walls, to visit a Tunisian scholar known throughout the Arab world. We stopped at a low, nail-studded door and clapped the iron knocker. Instantly the door was opened by a little coloured boy in crimson velvet, who flashed us a dazzling white and black smile and bowed us in. We stepped from the sunlight into a cool, dark courtyard paved with white marble; a fountain played in the centre, and in one corner a fig tree cast a green shade. The red and black page led us to an even darker room off the court and left us after lighting the dusk with

Tunisian woven mats have been famous for centuries.

another smile. As my pupils widened, I saw that the walls of the room were covered with blue and green tiles and the ceiling was of carved and painted wood. Under our feet lay a Persian carpet in tawny shades, and round the room ran a low cushioned bench covered with brocade and set at regular intervals with round wooden tables. Dominating the room was a huge, gilt-framed mirror in a style I recognised by now as old Venetian work for the oriental trade. It hung on the wall far above eye-level, its cloudy face reflecting nothing.

There was the opening and closing of a door, and Sidi Mahmoud's wife appeared. Roxane had told me that she was Turkish and a second wife, and I had pictured something along the lines of an odalisque. Madame Zeineb was in fact a handsome, dignified woman in middle age, dressed in a dark tailored suit. Only her eyes were blackened in an eastern way.

She and Roxane embraced wordlessly with the sad tender look between them of women who had seen many things. Roxane presented me.

Madame Zeineb gave me her hand with the palm downward, as ladies do who are used to having it kissed. "Roxane has told me about you." Her French was perfect with an oriental huskiness in her voice. "My husband is anxious to meet you."

She rang and a little black girl appeared, dressed in the same crimson livery, and carrying a tray of glasses in silver cuffs and a plate of tiny cakes, white, green, and red—the Tunisian colours.

In a moment Sidi Mahmoud glided in like a frail white butterfly. His thin form was draped in a snowy linen *gondourah* that fell from his wrists to the floor like a pair of wings. His face was seamed and yellow, his gestures precise and fine, and he spoke almost in a whisper. Yet his wife fell silent when he entered the room, and I could feel Roxane adjust to his presence.

We drank syrupy tea and ate the perfumed cakes. Sidi Mahmoud had just returned from Cairo where, along with other academicians, he had wrestled with the third or fourth letter of the Arabic alphabet. I had studied just enough Arabic to break down my resistance to semitic grammar, and said something he misinterpreted as intelligent.

"Come into the library," he suggested, and we left the ladies at tea.

Sidi Mahmoud had one of the finest collections of Arab books and manuscripts in Tunis. Many were beautiful objects— I remember one written in gold letters on a pale blue parchment—but my understanding of their contents, even of their titles, went only as far as deciphering a few letters. The pleasures of Arabic literature do not come lightly. My eyes kept straying to other objects, a collection of Persian miniatures scattered around the library like a pack of exquisite playing cards. The pleasures of the Persians are available to anyone, and I feasted on scenes of cruelty and lust of such refinement that they were no more disturbing than the passions of flowers. Sidi Mahmoud talked with the quiet excitement of a devotee, mentioning universities sunk in decay before those of Europe were founded, calibrating Christian and Hegira dates for me, and citing such medieval luminaries as Averroës, Ibn Battuta, and Ibn Khaldoun. I understood barely half: I was reflecting how his thin, almost transparent hands resembled the manuscripts they fondled and whose contents were written in the folds and wrinkles of his brain, while his soft voice and delicate gestures were like those of the hunters and lovers in the Persian miniatures.

As we left the library he handed me a book with the curious title *Prolegomena*. "He was an alumnus of our university here," he said; "that was in the 750's, the 14th century of your era. But Ibn Khaldoun will tell you a lot about Tunisia, then and now." The book was a French translation of the Arabic. I thanked him and we went back to the shadowy room off the courtyard. Roxane and Madame Zeineb sat there under the clouded gilt mirror, wrapped in a silence that was part of a conversation beyond my understanding.

If you are, as I was, completely ignorant of the name and achievement of Abu Zayid Abd al-Rahman ibn Muhammad ibn Khaldoun, no one can blame us. The founder of the modern science of history is hardly given the nod of a footnote in our histories. He was born in Tunis in the 1300's (*pace* Sidi Mahmoud, I will use Gregorian dates) and studied at the university there. He went to work at the palace but became involved in an intrigue against the ruler of Tunis and was forced to flee to Spain. In an age of despots, he was not noticeably loyal to any of them. He spent two years in prison in Morocco for a plot against the Sultan of Fez and, fleeing again from a plot against the Sultan of Tlemsin, he turned up as a teacher in Al-Azhar university in Cairo. In 1400 we find him negotiating a treaty between the Sultan of Egypt and Tamerlaine in Damascus. He knew the world of his time, and it was perhaps his insights into politics that inspired him both to his disloyalties and his theories of history.

The *Prolegomena* is a revelation, a precursor of Viço, Spengler, Toynbee and other philosophers of history. Ibn Khaldoun refused to accept history as either divine Revelation or the caprice of princes. Every society, he decided, is the product of forces that operated in the past, and to understand a society it is necessary to find out what those forces were. He discovered three laws: the law of causality which operates in the affairs of men as it does in nature; the law of resemblance, "Human nature is uniform because of the common origin of mankind. There are certain constants in humanity which are met with everywhere and always, which means that the present is a criterion for judging the past"; and the law of differentiation, by which climate, geography, and even diet may influence

the economic and political life, the beliefs and morality of
a society.

These are accepted ideas today, but like many common-
places they were revolutionary when Ibn Khaldoun pro-
pounded them. (It is interesting to note that, if anyone in 14th-
century Europe had been capable of propounding them, he
might very well have been reduced to cinders.) Ibn Khaldoun
also held a cyclical theory of history long before the modern
prophets of doom. He saw that states, like men, have their
periods of youth, virility, maturity, and old age, and thought
that the cycle lasted about 120 years in each case. But the idea
that most struck me in the *Prolegomena* was the medieval
Tunisian's awareness of the interpenetration of cultures and
civilisations. In the continual rise and fall of dynasties and
states, he noted that the conqueror sometimes destroys an
entire civilisation and imposes his own forms and patterns on
the vanquished society. But he also noted that the conqueror
frequently adopts the civilisation of the vanquished because
he finds it superior to his own. O Ibn Khaldoun, I called
across the centuries, things haven't changed much in your
home town; I wish you were here to talk them over.

The University of Zeitounia, or the Olive Tree, where Ibn
Khaldoun studied, was planted in Tunis about 1100 years ago
and still flourishes there. I used to skirt its walls near the Souk
al-Attarine and see the pale, serious students in their black
wool *gondourahs* waiting on the porch between classes. But I
could not enter, for the Zeitounia is a mosque as well as a
school. When I did meet some of the students, I found their
minds a curious mixture of medieval learning and up-to-the-
minute politics. The curriculum was rigidly Koranic, but
attached to the university was an institute named in honour of
the most illustrious alumnus. The Khaldounia was appropriately a more modern, secular adjunct to the university. The
students wore shirts and trousers and studied, among other

things, modern languages. I once precipitated a minor crisis in Protectorate politics when, at the request of some of the students, I helped them set up a course in English. But the closest I got to these centres of learning was the library, a building apart in an old Turkish barracks, and of this I remember most clearly a courtyard with an upper gallery of dazzling white and black striped arches and the fact that the books, regardless of subject or language, were shelved according to size.

I became better acquainted with another cultural spring in the Medina, the Rashidiya, a conservatory of Arab music. To most western ears Arab music sounds like caterwauling—and my ears are no different. But most Arab music is trash from the Tin Pan Alleys of Cairo and Damascus, no better than the stuff from Hollywood or Broadway by which it is heavily influenced. The Rashidiya was created to preserve, and compose, classic Arab songs and orchestral pieces, especially those of Andalusia, the North African Arab's lost paradise in Spain. Though flecked with quarter notes and coloured with bizarre harmonies, Andalusian music was not only comprehensible to my ears but enjoyable in its own context. Oddly enough this conservatory of ancient modes was in the care of youth: it was directed by three brothers, one a fledgling lawyer, the others still students, and the orchestra was composed largely of their classmates from the Khaldounia or the French Institute in the new city. Several of the players were Jews, who are much in demand at Tunisian women's parties where Moslem males are not allowed. Because of the trace of disreputability that clings to music-making in the Arab world, many of the players, including the three brothers, used pseudonyms for their concerts and broadcasts. I used to drop into the old unused palace where they played as often as I could and was pleasantly struck by the contrast between the shirt-sleeved enthusiasm of the young musicians and the ancient music in an

33

ancient place. They had a number of guest singers, the best of them an old harridan with a tragic mask of a face who sang the laments for Andalusia as if her heart would break. A younger girl sometimes took her place; each week her belly became fuller and fuller until it was clear that she was pregnant; there was a great joke among us that the entire orchestra was the father. After the concerts I sometimes went home with the three brothers for supper and long discussions of music, sex, and politics, the latter two being the chief preoccupations of the young Tunisian male.

The Old City is at its best during the nights of Ramadan. Ramadan is the Arab Lent, a whole month in the Islamic year when good Moslems fast all day, abstaining from food, drink, tobacco, medicines, and sex during the daylight hours. In Tunisia the people make up for lost time at night, and carnival reigns in the Old City from shortly after sunset to an hour or two before dawn. The religious leaders frown on the nocturnal revelry as inappropriate to the solemnity of Ramadan, and for two years the festivities were suspended during Tunisia's fight for independence. But the people love them, and as public opinion forces even the lukewarm Moslem to keep the daytime fast, it has forced the religious to accept the fun at night.

The Moslem year is ten days shorter than the sun's, so the Arab months creep slowly through the seasons. Ramadan was in summer when I arrived in Tunisia. The rich might sleep during the day, but the poor had to work as usual. As the long hot days dragged on, their eyes became shot with blood, the breath from their dry mouths grew foul, tempers frayed and fighting flickered and flared in the street. Even non-Moslems avoided smoking in public or sitting in a sidewalk café for fear of giving offence. When the sunset gun boomed from the Kasbah and the voice of prayer issued from minaret and radio, all of Tunis felt relieved. The Moslems sipped a

Tunis—street scene in the Old City

little lemonade or a cup of soup, lit the first cigarette, and prepared to sit down to their first meal.

A few hours later they were out in search of entertainment. Families of bourgeois, bevies of white shrouded women, portly gentlemen in gold flecked turbans and embroidered robes, pale students from the Zeitounia, gangs of young toughs, bedouin in from the *bled,* and everywhere streaks of children, filthy and in rags—all bent on the simple pursuit of pleasure, moved toward Halfaween, a gay, slummy quarter that was the focus of the fun.

First a turn around the square to look over the choice of pleasures. There are magicians, gambling games, puppet shows, concerts, belly dancers, and carts and counters of holiday food and drink. The noise is pandemonic: the shouts of hawkers swoop round your head, conflicting strains of music overlap as you walk. The wandering coffee vendor clicks his cups like castanets and fills them by tilting the urn on his back. Liquids of unearthly hue—yellow as pencils, red as medicine, green as a dye—are ladled out of fish-bowls. Trays of bright coloured sweets, some like sweaty orange worms, others like pale pink powder-puffs, all so sweet they give you toothache. The smell of the fry-shops is irresistible or nauseating depending on your liver.

The games of chance are a transparent hoax that take in only the youngest ragamuffin or most wide-eyed bedouin. The magicians' tricks are a little more opaque, but their impudent spiels are worth the small admission. If you are lucky you may find a puppet show—Karakouz they are called after the main character, a lecherous cross between Punch and Marius. Karakouz is a Turkish import, now naturalised in Tunisia. He was outlawed by the French, and refined Tunisians mention his name with embarrassment. You will see why.

Some Tunisian friends took me to see one my second Ramadan. It was hidden in an alley; some street urchins guided us to it. We bought them tickets and they crowded into the small room with us. On the rear benches a few women sat giggling behind their veils in anticipation. The tiny stage was covered with a sheet, and it is the shadow of the puppets on this screen that the audience sees—an aesthetic device the Restoration playwrights would have appreciated, for by being twice removed from reality, first by puppets and then by shadows, the enormities of Karakouz are made laughable and even emblematic. The dialogue spoken by the unseen puppeteers is outrageous.

In the show I saw the Pasha is just off to fight the Infidel. (Cheers from the street urchins who loudly identify the Infidel.) He leaves Karakouz to look after his wife, who stands demurely by. The Pasha perorates on his confidence in Karakouz, the untrustworthiness of women left unguarded, and what he will do to the Infidel and to anyone he catches tampering with his wife. (Giggles from the ghosts in the back row.) Karakouz makes gestures, all highly comical, of agreement, surprise, fear, and impatience as the Pasha rattles on. The Pasha almost leaves several times, but to Karakouz' growing chagrin he pops back again and again to repeat his threats and admonitions. At last he bestrides his horse, which rises up from the pit, and gallops off to kill infidels. Karakouz anticipates another return (the children scream with suspense)—and then bestrides the Pasha's wife. I think she protests a little, but in the mêlée of thrashing limbs on the screen it is hard to tell struggle from passion. And in the general hubbub of the audience it is impossible to distinguish her cries from ours.

The Pasha returns! (Shouts of warning from the audience.) Karakouz doesn't see him and continues with his work. Whack! goes the Pasha's sword on Karakouz' behind. Whack! whack! goes the Pasha's sword all over the place. The wife screams and jumps into the pit. The Pasha's curses are rich and juicy, Karakouz' screams delicious to our ears.

Blackout. Second act. Karakouz is discovered mournfully crossing the desert on a broken-down camel. He bemoans his exile and swears he will never —— a woman again. (I'm afraid that's the kind of language he uses.) The camel grows wearier and wearier. Karakouz thrashes it. The camel falters, falls, and rolls over, its legs in the air. Karakouz beats and curses the carcass. He looks at it from the head. He looks at it from the rear. An idea dawns. With a yell of triumph, Karakouz —— s the camel. Blackout.

The women wipe away tears of merriment with the corner of their veils. The little children stream out in a transport of delight.

But the principal mystery of Halfaween nights was the *concert oriental*. Now, an oriental concert has little in common with concerts as we know them, or if it has it is only the first step on the road to sublimation. The heavily accented music, the plaintive yearning of the singers, the orgiastic movements of the belly dancers are all frankly erotic. A generation ago, Tunisian men never saw a strange woman unveiled without paying for it, and even fifteen years ago the sight of an Arab woman's face had the thrill of rarity—like that of fresh strawberries before deep-freezing deprived us Americans of it. The singers and dancers of Halfaween were not all beautiful, but they had that quality of sexual awareness, of flagrant femaleness that flowers in a segregated society. Modes of sensuality differ among different people, but artificiality seems to be a universal lure of Venus: the painted cheek, the bound foot, the blondes that gentlemen prefer. Tunisians like their artificiality laid on thick. Brides, belly dancers, even respectable housewives of the old school paint a conventionalised mask across their honest features, with eyebrows curving down to the cheek-bone and eyelids flashing like silver fish in a green sea. *Kohl,* from which comes our word "alcohol" but which is really an antimony dye, is used to thicken and blacken each lash, causing the eyeballs to shine like mirrors. Fingers and palms are often stained with henna, and beauty spots are thick as raisins in a pudding. Unlike their brash Egyptian sisters, Tunisian belly dancers are fully clothed, their dresses of satin liberally sprinkled with sequins where emphasis is desired. The dancers add a touch of boudoir intimacy by constantly making small adjustments of shoulder straps, hairpins, and other items of feminine engineering.

The belly dance itself is constructed on the principal of isolation. The entire body comes into the act, but each part does its stint separately as if a spotlight were thrown on it. The spotlight is movement. The arms, head, shoulders, breasts, belly, hips all take their turn, while the rest of the body stands by, as it were, like the *corps de ballet* watching the ballerina. Some of the movements are based on coition, either standing or bending from the knees backwards. Others are feats of balance or exhibitions of disjointedness. The beat of the music is constantly changing and the pace of the dancer's movements changes with it. Often the rhythm shifts three or four times in a single number, usually in increasing tempo. The end of each piece is like an orgasm.

The reaction of a Tunisian audience to all this titillation seems passive. The men sit puffing a water pipe or sipping *orgeat* or tea. Occasionally one will sigh or mutter a phrase of admiration and wonder. But applause is rare and a western innovation. The passivity is deceptive. The concert is long, and after an hour or two of listening the rhythm enters a man's blood and his pulse keeps time to it. The abrupt changes are almost physically painful, the quickening of the beat unbearably exciting. Each hearer gets up and leaves when he wishes. But the rhythms stay with him and when he tries to sleep the pounding of his blood demands release in desire. This physiological effect is one of the secrets of the belly dance.

Each year at Halfaween there were several dancers, ranging

from the wonderfully adept old troupers who performed in temporary shacks crowded with working men and bedouin, to the glamorous stars from Cairo or Algiers whose names were billed outside the theatres and garden cafés that catered to students and others who could afford the higher admission. The first year I was in Tunisia, one of these stars was an American, daughter of a Miss C—— from Baltimore and an unknown father who was believed to be a Tunisian musician. Aïsha, as she was called, spoke no English and had never been to the United States, but she maintained her nationality proudly. She even continued the patriotic tradition by producing a child of her own, paternity also doubtful, and therefore an American citizen too.

The following year the undisputed queen of Halfaween was a dancer named Jamila. Jamila was Tunisian, unusually tall for an Arab girl, with long legs and hips shaped like a violin. Unlike most belly dancers, who are sultry to the point of sullenness, Jamila smiled continually, a great ravishing smile as if she enjoyed her work. Her cheek had the downy blush of a ripe peach—her flesh was firm as an apple's—her mouth looked like a dark, over-ripe plum: Jamila called for such images of the earth's abundance. I went several times to the café where she danced and could have arranged to meet her, for some of my friends from the Rashidiya were in the orchestra. But during that month of Ramadan, I was taken up with an American girl who was passing through. She was the opposite of Jamila in every way—blonde, dry, boyish—and I remember thinking how generous it is of nature to provide both fruit and sweet corn for our enjoyment.

After the American had left I went back to the café. Ramadan was over and the stage had been dismantled. A few old men sat at the tables listening to the bleat of an Arab radio. I asked the proprietor where I could find the dancer, and he gave me the name of an impasse in a poor section of the Medina.

There was a single door in the impasse. I knocked.

"Who?" called a woman's voice in the Arab fashion of answering doors and telephones. It is a question I find hard to answer: who I am often depends on who I'm talking to.

"An American," I tried. "I want Jamila, the dancer."

There was a long silence. My Arabic was not up to a fuller explanation, so I repeated my errand.

At last I heard the clank of a bolt and the door cracked open. A kohl-rimmed eye peered out at me. Then the crack widened. In the shadow was an old woman dressed in the ancient Tunisian house-dress of a sleeved brassière and long striped *foutah*, or towel, wrapped round the hips.

"She is not here," the old woman said. "She has gone away."

"Where?"

"The Lord knows."

"Will she be back?"

"If God wills."

I thought I'd force His hand. "Can you send for her?" I asked.

This released a torrent of words beyond my understanding. People often say they can understand a foreign language but not speak it. My experience has usually been the opposite.

"Peace, my mother," I said. "I want to see her very much. Jamila is beautiful." The word *jamila* in Arabic means beautiful. My expression, which might have been meaningless, made the old woman smile.

"Peace to you, my son," she said. "I will tell her," and she closed the door.

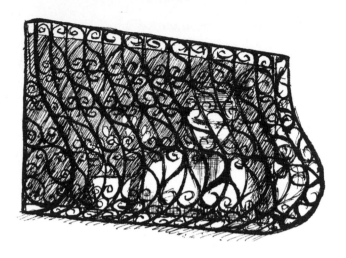

II. SIDI-BOU-SAÏD

THE FIRST TIME I VISITED SIDI-BOU-SAÏD—THE WHITEWASHED
village on the cliff which the White Father had called a suburb
of Carthage—I decided to live there.

As you drive out from Tunis, you see the town surging up
the hillside to break on the cliff's edge like a wave of the sea,
the houses white as foam, the minaret and lighthouse hanging
in the air like the highest drops of spray. From within, the
village also suggests a marine origin, its form fluid but com-
pact, its design organic, the houses growing out of one another,
putting out rooms and wings that turn into a street or a new
neighbourhood by a process of accretion like the homes of
those sea animals that expand from a single cell to an entire
atoll. The streets and footpaths wander through like the track
of a snail, leisurely and impromptu, stopping in *culs-de-sac*,
tunnelling under the houses, or breaking off abruptly at the
cliff. The doors and windows of the houses are painted sea-
blue or -green. Many of the villagers are fishermen and at

night you see their oil-soaked torches where they wander with sack and trident looking for succulent octopus among the rocks, like yellow glow-worms reflected in the dark water at the foot of the cliffs.

Sidi–bou–Saïd is a holy town. My lord the Father of Saïd, which is what the name means, was one of those saints or *marabouts* through whom the Moslems of North Africa temper the awful One-ness of God. Their tombs, also known as marabouts, dot the landscape with little white domes; over some of them great mosques have been built; others grow into whole towns or villages, like Sidi–bou–Saïd. This *marabout*, like the more efficient Christian saints, demonstrated his holiness by working useful, unspectacular miracles, like eliminating rheumatism from the neighbourhood and forbidding scorpions to sting near his shrine. Sidi–bou–Saïd then is also a healthy place to live. The villagers know this and consider themselves blessed above the surrounding towns. The saint's grace—the health, the holiness, and the pride—is visibly manifest in the extraordinary beauty of the place.

This owes much to the situation, a promontory north of Tunis where the bay curves from the civilised shore of Carthage and suddenly opens to the wide, wild sweep of Tunisia's northern coast. Landward the eye soars over the rooftops, across a tawny, olive-tufted plain to the buried ruins of Carthage and the modern towns on the rim of the lake, which dispose themselves with that well-known peculiarity of Mediterranean landscapes into an illustration for a history of western civilisation. The view of the bay looks down on the opaque, blue-grey or violet water wrinkled by ships and fishing boats, and across at the horizontal coast of Cap Bon, striated pink and brown, where the volcanic cone of Bou Kornine ("Double Horned") and Jebel Rassas ("Mountain of Lead") shoulder each other against the sky. The sea-view is pure and untrammelled, without detail or limit, only the colours

of water and sky changing constantly, but most characteristic-
ally a deep blue-green, the colour of the Madonna's robe—
what Spengler calls the Catholic colour of infinity.

The town is worthy of the setting, its accidental loveliness
miraculously preserved from improvements and modernisa-
tion. The white cubistic drawing of the houses is intact. The
blue and green doors fade to a distant sea colour; a few are
carved with medallions and picked out in sherbet colours of
pink, yellow, green; some are set in archways of black and
white marble blocks or soft yellow stone cut with arabesques;
the knockers are usually a woman's hand with lace cuff and
ring and holding an iron ball. The houses of Sidi-bou-Saïd
are not blind like those of Tunis, but they wear veils. Some of
these are grilles that curve outwards and down in a pendant
shape like half a fig or a woman's heavy breast, the flat bottoms
holding pots of herbs and flowers and permitting women to
look down on the street with their faces partly hidden. More
elaborate veils are the *mesharabiyyah*, projecting balconies of
close lattice work where women may sit in comfort and
decency to watch the world outside. Round every corner is
an unexpected grace: a fig tree growing high on a wall, a
column from one of the pasts of Carthage re-employed, a
black iron lantern like a cage for nightingales. The stairways
that climb the steeper streets of town have stone balustrades to
keep children and animals from falling into the view. A shawl
of purple bougainvillea or the dark points of cypress trees
indicate a garden behind the walls.

After long search, and with the help of Roxane, I found a
house that pleased me, even if it did not exactly fit like a glove.
Arabs use their living space differently from ours, their main
concern being privacy, that luxury of the very rich in our
world. My house was a self-contained compound of courtyards, terraces, and very few rooms, enclosed in a windowless
wall ten feet high. A huge stone arch faced the street; this was

filled in with thick wooden doors, which were rarely opened; you entered through a small square opening cut in the side, so high and small you had to lift your feet and duck your head to pass through. You stepped into a forecourt planted with jasmine, geraniums, and seven cypress trees. On the left a door led to the square, high vaulted room where an Arab gentleman would receive visitors. On the right was the *harim*, a word signifying privacy, a suite of tiny rooms, each a step or two higher or lower than the last, with windows only on the courtyards, and behind them a large empty cube over the cistern where the women, children, and female servants would work and play under the open sky. A narrow flight of steps led to the roof where a terrace of several levels, corresponding to the rooms below, looked out over the sea and bay. I fitted myself into this foreign space as well as I could, rather enjoying the incongruity and adaptation. As it was summer, I first furnished the roof with mats and cushions and low tray-like tables, and lay like Michel in the first chapter of *The Immoralist*, gazing out over a miniature world.

My first caller was a neighbour who introduced himself with a note of professional pride as "Beshir ben ——, the artist." At first I thought he was a child, not only on account of his slight stature and a tousled thatch of black hair, but also because of an open, unguarded look and uncomplicated manner as if he had not yet donned adult armour. He was in fact only a few years younger than I. After a greeting so casual I thought we had met before, he began to wander about my house with an air of deep abstraction. I am no handyman, and my attempts to cope with Tunisian wiring and plumbing made the original makeshifts look like the work of a graduate engineer. Beshir offered to help. I accepted and thereby incurred one of the biggest debts of my life. Arab generosity has no limits, and once you have contracted friendship with one of them, you

Hand-carved stone in traditional designs is still a feature of present-day architecture.

are in the red for life. Beshir's introduction of himself had been an understatement: he was not only a painter, but also an architect, mason, carpenter, electrician, and fabricator of imaginative fancies of plaster, wire, glass, or whatever lay at hand. Behind his air of abstraction was a passionate interest in materials and technique. He put all his talents at my disposal, and soon my house became the perfect setting for a bachelor —a little rococo, a little cock-eyed, a sort of heavenly *pied-à-terre*.

I soon learned that Beshir was Andalusian. That is, his ancestors were among the Arabs who had driven the Goths out of Spain and kept the Dark Ages from crossing the Pyrenees. After seven hundred years they themselves had been driven back into Africa by Ferdinand and Isabella. His family still possessed the deeds to their Spanish properties and the key to their house in Cordova. Beshir used to sing the Andalusian songs, strumming a guitar or improvising a rhythm on a box of matches or a handful of coins. They were all plaintive, full of yearning for the lost paradise of Spain, and invariably ended in a wordless sob of grief. He also wrote poetry about imaginary worlds across the sea, or sometimes under it, inhabited by persecuted maidens and luckless heroes. Beshir himself had a series of French and Jewish girl friends when I knew him, but his heart belonged to a cousin he had not seen since childhood.

Beshir's Tunisia was as fabulous as the golden plains of Andalusia. Most Arabs have a pragmatic attitude toward facts: they are not true so much as attractive or helpful, not false so much as disloyal or unseemly. This gives them a warm, partisan colouration, unlike the cold grey products of the scientific mind. Beshir's version of the external world was the result of an inner vision, a product of the selective eye. He could spot a Vandal face in the street, or trace the line of classic Greece in the dress of a bedouin girl. Once he took me to two dusty country towns, Testour and Tebourba, which had been settled by Moslem refugees from Spain, and we searched for traces of Spanish art and the pathos and grandeur of exile. Another time we visited a noisy corner of Tunis, a junction of tram lines scoring the ground with tracks and the sky with wires; to Beshir it was a shrine, for behind a grimy wall covered with tattered signs was the tomb of one of the last Arab kings of Spain. Beshir's Tunisia was inhabited by these ghosts and by a living race of noble fishermen, blacksmiths, farmers, and *marabouts*. The clerks and politicians, mechanics and shopkeepers of modern Tunis were invisible to him.

Beshir lived on the roofs of Sidi-bou-Saïd at the top of a long flight of stairs. Viewed simply as a means of getting up and down, the stairway seemed eccentric and perverse: it meandered as casually as the streets outside, changing direction and gradient, pausing at unmotivated landings, opening into ledges, niches, and cubby-holes that were something between cupboards and rooms. The reasons for this lay in the houses on either side. Arab domestic architecture is not formal, but organic; doors are cut, windows walled up, rooms added or subtracted as the need arises. In a few generations a house holds traces of buried archways and forgotten entrances like the ghosts of former inhabitants. Beshir's staircase had been part of previous arrangements, its oddities reminders of prior existence. The penthouse in which he lived had sprouted in answer to some new need; it was a single big room that served him as studio, bedroom, salon, and storehouse. There were windows on every side, and the neighbours' roofs served as a terrace. His view swept the entire horizon.

Both penthouse and stairway were choked with evidence of Beshir's love of materials and form, his country, and the sea. Every ledge and cranny contained flotsam and jetsam of his past and present preoccupations: shells, branches of coral, frail husks of sea horses, the articulate spine of a sole, deformed

shards and sea-worn handles of clay pots (his "phalli collection" he called them); a weathered ram's horn; glass balls
used to float fishing nets and the nets themselves dyed tobacco
brown by the brine; tools, gear, tackle, and trim of his friends
the artisans; and a collection of simple household objects worn
by generations of hands like the glass and shards by the sea.
These objects appeared like beloved children over and over in
his paintings. Beshir was no primitive: he had studied in Paris,
but his best pictures had the look of things seen for the first
time, almost before their meaning was grasped, with the bloom
of wonder still on them—the irridescent scales of a fish or a
pigeon's neck, black seeds floating in the pink chalice of a
watermelon, the taut pattern of threads on a loom. The
Mediterranean usually appeared in the background, and his
brush was dipped in its infinite colours. The horizon was often
closed by the cone of Bou Kornine, deep blue or violet, sometimes pink in the tangential rays of the sun.

Beshir's stairs were also infested with Negroes. As you
climbed to the penthouse, a soft-piled voice greeted you
politely and a smile would lighten the shadow of a niche.
There were a couple of men, and one woman who ran the
household from a kitchen cranny at the foot of the stairs.
Beshir seemed unaware of the men's existence, but he called
the Negress "mama" and they embraced frequently and with
affection. She was good-looking, with black satin skin, plum-
coloured eyes, and an ample figure, dignified to the point of
haughtiness but capable of sudden bursts of mocking laughter,
and of an indeterminate age bordering on the motherly. As
Beshir was as white-skinned as I, I found the relationship
puzzling. Her name was Laila.

Soon after I knew him I mentioned to Beshir that I needed a
housekeeper, but he could suggest no one. That evening there
was a knock at my gate, and I opened the small side door to
find a white figure in the dusk.

"I have come to cook your supper," it said and stepped into the courtyard. When the *ha'ik* dropped I saw it was Laila.

"Did Beshir send you?" I asked.

"No," she grinned; "he's already eaten. One of the others will go if he needs anything." She strode to the kitchen as if she knew the way.

My larder was the limited one of a bachelor, but in half an hour Laila served me an excellent meal—a kind of salad-omelette of tomatoes, onions, green peppers and eggs cooked in olive oil, which in Arabic is called *shakshouka*. The dish was hot and peppery but with it Laila served bite-size chunks of melon to cool the palate. I was well satisfied and called her in with the coffee. She sat down at the table and over two cups we discussed the terms of my surrender.

Beshir seemed unaware of the new relationship, and when I tried to tell him he shrugged it off as no concern of his. I was out most of the day; the housework was done in my absence, and my supper was ready when I got home. At first I tried to make Laila do things my way, and she obliged with good-humoured condescension. As dishes had to cross an open courtyard between the kitchen and table, I told her always to heat the plates. She forgot for a while, but on one occasion triumphantly set out plates too hot to touch—then served a cold dinner on them. I soon stopped interfering and little by little my household became Arabised.

I dined on *couscous*—a mound of steamed semolina under a stew of lamb, chicken, or fish, with chickpeas, pumpkin, and other vegetables; or on *briques*—hot triangular pastries stuffed with chopped liver and a raw egg, then lightly fried, which you eat with your fingers and an agile sucking motion—a great trial to beginners; or on *meshwi* of broiled meat and organs of lamb on a spit; or on chicken, skinned and boned, and re-stuffed with two pastes, one of almond and one of pistachio, so it looks when cut like beige marble with green and white

48

veins. With these I ate purple olives prepared at home, fried sunflower seeds and pine nuts, *leban* like a thin yoghurt, rose-scented creams, and green and purple figs; melons red, gold, and pale green; amber and black dates; white grapes dusted with rust and long black grapes called "Negress' teats", and sweet lemons called *beldi*.

My life was Arabised in other ways. Laila made me a cool linen *gondourah* to wear in the house in summer, and bought me a camel-hair *burnous* to wear out of doors in bad weather. The *gondourah* is a sort of personal air-conditioner, a broad shirt that is all sleeve, falling from the wrists to the level of your knees, to let the air circulate over your entire body. The *burnous* on the other hand is a form of insulation. It is an over-coat, a raincoat, a blanket, and a tent. I have used mine as a bed of both over and under covers, and as a dressing room at the beach. Arabs in the country use theirs as portable privies. On horseback it shields the rider and a good part of the horse from whatever element is being hostile. Besides its utility it is a handsome, dramatic garment, falling in deep natural folds, not frozen in stiff pipes and panels like a suit. The Arabs wear it in different ways to indicate age, marital status, and profession. The *burnous* is one of the great, simple sartorial inventions, like the beret and the T-shirt.

Laila hired a boy to clean my house and kept after him with the passion for cleanliness of a Swiss housewife. She herself was immaculate and took almost voluptuous care of her person. After she had been with me a while I noted a heavy con-sumption of sugar and lemons and asked her about it: she used them, it seems, in a secret rite to remove all the hairs from her body. Scented oils were also part of her toilet, and at least once a week she went to the *hammam*, or public baths.

Every nation, I think, believes itself to be cleaner than all others, and each has its own symbol of cleanliness. Ours is the daily bath and efficient garbage collection: the French swear by the *bidet*; in oriental countries great importance is attached to removing street shoes before entering a building. The Arabs' symbol is the *hammam*. Until lately only the richest Tunisians had bathrooms in their homes, and even today many houses do not contain a tub. The *hammam* is both a social and a sanitary institution. Even Tunisians who possess the most modern plumbing still go to the *hammam* on special occasions—before weddings or holidays—and periodically to get "clean under the skin."

As every nation is convinced of its own immaculateness, we seem also to be blind to dirt outside our own system. The Arabs have a peculiar tolerance for filth in the streets. We Americans—but let me repeat a conversation I once had with Beshir.

"Is it true," he asked "that Americans use toilet paper?"

"Of course," I replied, unseeing.

"Is that all? Do you *only* wipe?"

"Yes. What do you expect us to do?"

He did not hide his disgust. "Wash of course, as we do. Even the French are cleaner than you."

Beshir was fond of *hammams* because he said they were direct descendants of Roman baths and hence part of the Arabs' classical heritage. One early morning he called for me and we walked down the hill to a neighbouring village that had an old and famous *hammam*. It was in a long white building, with one end blackened by the fires below. We entered at the other end into a spacious hall with pillars supporting a vaulted ceiling, and an ornate fountain in the centre. Along the walls ran a platform covered with mattresses, and above them hung latticed cabinets for our clothes. We undressed, wrapping cotton *foutahs* round our hips (the Arabs are extreme prudes about exposing their bodies even before their own sex) and slipped our feet into wooden clogs several inches high. Then we entered the hot rooms.

There are three of these, growing progressively hotter and

Sidi-bou-Saïd from the air

steamier. You spend several minutes in each to accustom your body gradually to the rising temperature. Bath attendants, also in *foutahs* and clogs, throw buckets of water on the stone floor to raise the steam. If it were not for the clogs, you could not stand on the griddle-hot floor. In the last room, directly over the fires and where the atmosphere is opaque with steam, there was a small pool of nearly boiling water. I dipped a foot in gingerly, but braver men than I lower their whole bodies by painful degrees. After a few minutes here you feel your flesh beginning to melt like tallow.

Once the pores are open, the sweat flowing, and the flesh malleable, you move back to the slightly less torrid atmosphere of the second room and lie down on a platform like a lump of obedient clay. The masseur and washer, usually an old man with skin like a sponge but muscles like an *écorché*, takes over. With a harsh glove he scrapes your hide from scalp to toe, stripping off dead skin and engrained dirt in rolls which are called 'candle wicks.' If you wish he will wash your head with a special pink-brown mud that leaves the hair glossy and sweet smelling. Then comes the exquisite torture of an Arab massage. There is the usual universal pinching, pommelling, kneading, and joint cracking, but it is all performed with a trance-like rhythm that makes your mind as supine as your body. And it ends with a special refinement: the masseur, squatting, *walks* down your spine, letting the soles of his feet slide along your ribs with a slap to the ground. After this you are sent to a small cell with running water and a razor where you wash your private parts and—another symbol to the Arabs—shave them. Then, completely enfolded in three fresh *foutahs*, you proceed to the least hot of the three rooms and, when you've cooled down enough, to the dressing-room, where you lie on your mattress as long as it takes you to recover. I felt cleaner than I had ever been in my life before and, when I reached the street, as if I were walking an inch or two above the ground.

I soon got to know other neighbours and friends in Sidi-bou-Saïd.

Muhammad the carpenter, a good craftsman but inclined to go off on fantasies of his own if left unwatched (I could never think of enough things to tell him *not* to do, and his imagination was fertile). When I had known him about a year, he chucked his job one day and set off for Mecca. He had only a little money, so he went on foot. He reckoned it would take the rest of his life (he was about forty) to complete the pilgrimage, stopping to work and earn a little on the way.

The Baroness, widow of a Jewish financier of German origin, French title, and international fortune, who had come to Tunisia half a century ago, fallen in love with the Arabs (he wore Arab dress and wrote a four volume work on Andalusian music), settled here and did much to preserve the beauty of Sidi-bou-Saïd. She was a frail white wraith—white skin, white hair, white lace, and flowing white *burnous*—living alone in the palace her husband had built, a museum of Arabian architecture climbing half way down the cliff on terraces of black cypress and mauve geraniums that framed a stunning view of the bay—a haunted vision of Maxfield Parrish.

The village idiot, a gangling youth, fully dressed from the waist up but, because of incontinence, diapered in burlap rags which the bad boys of the village liked to unpin and snatch away from him to be chased with animal screams.

Naji, an ex-shepherd whom Laila hired for a while to work in my house. He had dark skin and crowded, sunburned hair, and looked like a mutilated bronze statue dug up at Carthage, for he had found a hand-grenade in a field one day and lost an eye, half a hand, and deep gouges of flesh over his face and body. He was touchy and sulked and, after several absences, finally disappeared altogether.

Catous, "The Cat," another short-lived houseboy, who took hashish and began wearing Laila's cast-off dresses. When one of Beshir's friends asked him if it was true he was pregnant, Catous replied, "Certainly not! I had the curse two days ago."

The princes of Sidi-bou-Saïd, cousins of the Bey and somewhere fairly high in line to the throne. The father and most of the sons were tall and blond, with military bearing and a simple charm that fluttered the hearts of the women in the village. The youngest son, who was my friend, was dark-haired and had a crooked spine; he ran the family enterprises that supported the indolent, carefree seductions of his brothers.

Laila began to spend more and more time at my house, and we used to sit for hours talking in one of the courtyards—or rather she talked in long inconsequential monologue, as she rolled out *couscous* or ironed Beshir's and my shirts, and I tried to write or paint. She spoke in French, with an occasional Arabic word or phrase, and at first I pondered over her odd erosions of both languages. Then I learned she was illiterate and spoke as it were phonetically. She had picked up some Saint Germain-des-Prés *argot* from Beshir and his painter friends, and mixed it oddly with literal translations of patriarchal phrases from the Koran. As with all Moslems, God was in her mouth all day, His name worn by use to a polite phrase or a mere intensive. "May God bless you" meant only thanks; "if God wills" was the equivalent of "I hope so"; and every other phrase was preceded by a fervent "By God". Mixed with invocations of deity was the peculiar Tunisian tolerance of obscenity, so widespread and socially innocuous that I have heard parents use it to their children. Laila's speech was therefore a rich *shakshouka* of diverse elements.

Little by little I learned the nature of her relationship with Beshir. Laila had been one of those little serving children, like those I had seen at Sidi Mahmoud's house and elsewhere, and had grown up in Beshir's home. She did not remember her own parents, though she had a faint recollection of a man, possibly an uncle or a guardian, who had brought her to Tunis from the desert oasis where she was born. Like all great Tunisian families of that time, Beshir's parents had a large and variegated household—unmarried nephews and cousins, a divorced aunt or sister, and a number of unrelated individuals like Laila. Laila was a little older than Beshir's oldest sister, and grew up as her companion, servant, and, for a short unfruitful while, schoolmate. Beshir's mother had taught her housework, cooking, and sewing along with her own daughters. When Beshir was born, she became his nurse.

I had heard stories of the survival of slavery in the Arab world and wondered whether Laila, and the serving children I saw today, could be considered to be slaves. I questioned her.

"Did they pay you wages?"

"Lord no! Did they pay their own children?"

"Did they pay that man—the one that brought you to them —something for you?"

"How should I know? I don't even remember his face."

"Were you adopted?"

This meant nothing to her. I learned later that legal adoption is almost unknown among Moslems, and unnecessary due to their extended family feelings.

"Could you leave them if you wanted to?" I persisted.

"In the c— of thy mother!" she cried, exasperated, "where should I go? They were my family. I was their daughter. And now I am Beshir's mama."

It was clear that my categories, not hers, were blurred or needlessly rigid. Whatever her legal status, which I imagine was equivocal, Laila seemed to have been in the position of the devoted, privileged household slave of the *Arabian Nights* or the *ante-bellum* South. It didn't sound like a bad position to be in, the way she told it.

Laila had clearly been a favourite of Beshir's father. It was he who had given her the name Laila, which means "night", for like most Tunisian girls she had been named Fatma at birth. According to her, Beshir's father had been a saint and a scholar, a pillar of one of the brotherhoods of North African Islam. He often stayed up late at night reading the Koran or a pious commentary while the family slept. At those times he liked to have Laila sit in a corner of the study, sewing or knitting and ready to bring him a glass of tea or a coal for his water-pipe when needed. His wife remonstrated with him for keeping the girl awake and ordered Laila to bed. Laila refused, and mama beat her. As Laila told it, smiling reminiscently, she went to bed all right, but refused to get up again, to eat, or to speak to the family—until she was permitted to stay up as late as her master needed her. Laila spoke of Beshir's mother with affection, but not with the adoration she had for his father— and for Beshir.

Between the older couple there was a companionship that must have been rare in the sexually segregated society of their day. The family went to the seaside in summer, and papa liked to walk along the beach in the evening. Most Arabs prefer the male company of the sidewalks and cafés, but papa wanted his wife along. In those days, Tunisian women of the upper class never appeared in public places, even if heavily veiled. Beshir's father had the happy idea of dressing his wife as a boy and thus, arm in arm Tunisian male fashion, they strolled in the cool dusk. It must have been a rare opportunity for mama to see the world unfiltered through a veil or a latticed *mesharabiyyah*.

Beshir's parents died within a few months of each other while he was still a boy. His sisters had been married by that time, and on his deathbed papa said something that Laila construed as a sacred charge to look after the boy forever. Laila was already married herself. One of the rewards of the system of childhood service is a marriage arranged with a servitor of another rich family, and an expensive Moslem wedding. Laila even had children of her own—she forgot how many, as all but one had died at birth. Beshir was her true son, and she clung to him through thick and thin.

The male Negroes I encountered on Beshir's stairs were Laila's husband and son. The husband was a gentle, ineffectual man who went from job to job in the comfortable orbit of Tunisian nepotism. He drank, and frequently disappeared for a few days, coming back with no explanation but an apologetic smile, and moved back into a niche on the stairway, for Laila did not allow him in her room. When he badly needed another drink he took something of hers and sold it. Laila went before the *qadi* several times for a divorce, but she had no male relative to help her and Beshir maintained a lofty neutrality. Her son was a shy, wild adolescent, still reluctantly going to school. I felt sorry for both husband and son. She treated one with withering contempt and the other with a harsh watchfulness that might drive him down his father's damp path of rebellion. Laila's tender passages were all reserved for Beshir.

Laila was widely thought to be a witch. Though Arabs are supposed to be indifferent to race, they view Negroes with a mixture of humour and apprehension and credit them with occult powers brought from their native jungles. Laila enjoyed the status this gave her. She was an expert in the menstrual cycle and the secrets of fertility, and was much in demand among hopeful, or resentful, wives. She herself believed equally in the efficacy of blue beads, the Hand of Fatma, slippery elm, and the latest antibiotics. I once found my garden and doorway daubed with blood. When I questioned Laila she admitted she had sacrificed some creature to "keep you in Tunisia forever."

Alongside these atavistic prescriptions, Laila believed in and practised her religion in an accommodating, Mediterranean way. She went to the mosque on Fridays, told her beads, kept the fasts, eschewed pork and wine, and once made a sort of *novena* of prayers on successive days. My house was run on a

Moslem calendar. Thanksgiving or the Fourth of July might pass unnoticed, but not an anniversary of Muhammad or Fatma. Ramadan was kept more strictly than any Lent had been in my Catholic childhood. I made my own breakfast and went out to lunch, for Laila would prepare only the night-time meals. On the Feast of the Dead she rose at dawn and went to spend the day with Beshir's father and mother in the cemetery near Tunis. She took a picnic lunch and had plenty of company, as the cemeteries were filled with white-robed women that day. In the evening she returned with the latest gossip or a new recipe picked up among the tombs.

As the Feast of the Sacrifice approached, I was tactfully reminded of the high cost of sheep at that season. I suggested buying a lamb ahead of time, and giving it to a local shepherd to raise against the day, but this sort of anticipation was foreign to the Tunisian mind. Everyone bought an unblemished ram at inflated prices a few days before the feast, and the streets of the village were filled with bleating, bewildered animals tethered where they could fatten on refuse. I made the expected contribution on condition that the sacrifice was not to take place in my house. (I have never been able to see the religious virtue of bloodletting, but perhaps those who do know more about the nature of deity than I.) I was spared the sight of the ram alive and can only imagine it was kept tied on Beshir's stairway.

On the day itself, the brutes' throats are cut, part of the meat given to the poor, and the rest is roasted and eaten by each family. I was invited to join Laila's family gathering at noon but could not. However, I had asked some people, including Roxane and a couple of American girls, to dinner that night and as usual left the menu to Laila. I have never been able to decide whether she planned the meal as an honour or a joke. The stew for the *couscous* that evening consisted entirely of the sheep's organs, which are esteemed a great delicacy by the

Arabs. On top of the mound, arranged realistically and looking all too human, were the carefully preserved genitals of the ram.

Like all respectable Tunisian women, except the bedouin and a few very emancipated ladies at the other end of the social scale, Laila always wore a veil when she went out. She would not step into the street, even to go the few steps between Beshir's house and mine, without swathing herself from head to toe and, if the excursion were a long one or her hands too occupied to hold the cloth over her face, she strapped on a little black mask of silk as well. Indoors, she showed her face to anyone—friends, tradesmen, casual callers, whether Arabs or westerners. It was easy enough to recognise her under the *ha'ik* by her dark hands, her figure, or her walk, but if a casual male acquaintance spoke to her on the street she was affronted. The shopkeepers and street boys of Sidi-bou-Saïd knew this and used to call her politely by name, to provoke a blistering curse and indignant clutch of the veil. She was not entirely popular with the shopkeepers, for she drove a hard bargain and was a sharp critic of their ethics and their wares.

If the veil did not actually exist over large areas of the world, it would seem to be some wild invention of a Swift or Voltaire, designed to satirise our symbols of modesty. It is still a good *reductio ad absurdum* of any logical argument against nudism. There seems to be no real equivalent of the veil in our society. Although in stricter Moslem places and times, a woman's face and entire person might be assimilated to our idea of nakedness and that pawky phrase 'the privates', in Tunisian practice there is no similarity to our abolishment of certain parts of the body. As I have said, Laila showed her face to anyone indoors. In the street, Tunisian women often let the veil drop from their faces to rummage in handbags or adjust a parcel. I once saw a woman lower hers in a streetcar to restore her makeup. You are supposed not to look, but I was as incapable as Actaeon of not taking a fleeting glance. Some women wore veils only at certain places and times. The young and lovely wife of a *caïd* in a southern city used to appear at the theatre in Tunis protected only by diamonds, mink, and her own blinding beauty, but in the area of her husband's jurisdiction she ventured out only when swathed like a mummy and in a curtained car besides. Once at the airport I saw some rich Tunisians returning from a holiday in Paris, called back by a death in the family. The women came off the plane in smart Paris *tailleurs*, but they were met by relatives with extra *ha'iks* and as they reached the ground they wrapped themselves in the white shrouds.

One of the oddest styles in Tunis was the face-veil and head covering worn with otherwise European clothes. It sounds charming, like a domino or *mantilla*, but it is not: with the exhibitionism of western female dress, the blacked-out face looks prurient, like a fig leaf. There were even odder combinations. On the beach I saw a girl swimming in a complete head veil over a fairly revealing bathing suit. And at the foot of the cliffs at Sidi-bou-Saïd the village women sometimes bathed with their faces veiled, skirts plastered to their thighs, and breasts completely bare. They reminded me of the naked bather who, surprised by a party of women, instinctively covered his face.

If one could grasp all the nuances and contradictions of dress, one might understand the entire nature of society—perhaps even why we wear clothes at all. Diffidently, I advance a tentative explanation of the veil. Perhaps it is something like that thrilling element in fairy tales: the magic ring that renders its wearer invisible. An unveiled woman may be looked at or spoken to; she is part of the scene and must take the consequences. A woman who puts on a veil gives notice that she is to be considered not there. Even if the veil falls momentarily from her face, or if her breasts are bare, she is protected by the magic cap or ring or belt that grants invisibility. This may explain Laila's outrage when greeted in the street, and the double life of the *caïd*'s wife. There must be many occasions when it would be nice not to be visible, or recognised. Frenchwomen in Tunis were said to adopt the veil on amorous adventures, perhaps on the Bocaccian principle that a hidden sin is half forgiven. It was also a handy device for Arab men, whether patriots or felons, to escape detection.

All dress is ambivalent, a cunning pact between modesty and display. The Tunisian *ha'ik* is no exception. An attractive woman can contrive to show off her best points in it, and less favoured women must be grateful for the camouflage. A common seduction is to draw the cloth tight across the back and under the buttocks, which to the Tunisian male are the focus of voluptuousness that breasts are in the west. In some cases the *ha'ik* conceals about as little as the *draperie mouillée* in which Greek sculptors first revealed the female nude. In fact, the veil often seemed to me a survival of classicism, especially on Tunisian beaches when I saw veiled women or girls beside young men stripped to the briefest of French trunks, as on those Attic vases where draped nymphs and goddesses consort with naked heroes and gods. At other times, the image they called up was that of nuns in white habits. Both comparisons contain more than a visual resemblance: the segregation of sexes, 'taking the veil' at puberty, the role of women who live, not for themselves, but for their lord.

The veil, segregation, and the inequality of male and female did not desexualise Tunisian life. Far from it. Beshir's friends, students, painters, young men about Tunis, talked of little else. They satisfied their casual desires with French or Jewish girls, or, at a pinch, with native prostitutes. But these were only appetisers: their real hunger was for the invisible fruit that hung behind the *mesharabiyyas* and *ha'iks*. From Laila's reports of conversations on the other side of the veil, the same obsessions flourished there. Once in a while Laila brought a nice

Tunisian girl to my house and as a joke left her alone with me
for a few minutes. The girl was usually struck dumb with embarrassment, but the atmosphere of sexuality hung between us
as heavy as the scent of jasmine on the summer air. The veil is
now officially discouraged and Tunisian girls are urged to be
modern, i.e., masculine. It is sad to see other people following
our footsteps just when we are beginning to see, abashed,
where they have led.

Laila had grown up among the old families of Tunis, along
with Beshir's sisters and their friends, and now she was doubly
welcome in their homes as a purveyor of news and nostrums.
She frequently called on the wife of the Bey, an old friend and
useful in finding her husband a job between binges. Sometimes
she would come back from such visits and give me glimpses
into a strange, sequestered world.

I remember several weeks when she brought almost daily
bulletins on the trouble in one house. It involved greedy
parents, a headstrong girl, a preposterous suitor, and an arranged
marriage. I knew the girl's brother slightly and had seen the
suitor, so my interest was whetted. The suitor was Swiss and
elderly. He had arrived in Tunisia recently and let it be known
that he was very rich. Soon afterwards he announced his conversion to Islam, assumed Arab clothing, and began to seek a
Tunisian wife. I used to see him in the cafés and restaurants
of Tunis, wearing a *gondourah* and fez, in the company of the
kind of Tunisians who pick up rich foreigners—and who
would never dream of wearing Arab dress themselves. It was
probably one of these types that introduced him to the parents
of Aliya, the girl in the case. I never saw Aliya, but according
to Laila she was educated and looked like her brother, a dark-
haired boy with strongly chiselled features. The parents accepted the suit of the ridiculous Swiss, but Aliya did not. Laila
visited their home just after the first, and only, interview

between the old man and the girl, when she had rejected him. The mother and father were furious. Aliya locked herself in her room. The Swiss sat things out with his cronies in the Majestic Hotel bar.

Now, although marriages are traditionally arranged by parents in Islam, there is no power in Koranic law to force a girl into marriage against her will. Parents sometimes have powers of persuasion beyond the law, but Aliya had her own powers of resistance. Laila reported the stages in the struggle. The mother pleaded with the girl to think of her parents' happiness. The father threatened to withhold permission for her ever to marry anyone else. Aliya refused to unlock her door. The Swiss called on the parents again: he offered Aliya a diamond bracelet and her brother a job in a Swiss bank. Aliya went on a hunger strike. Laila, who had known the girl since she was born, begged her through the door to take some food, but whispered encouragement to her in the fight. I was afraid that Aliya, driven desperate, might kill herself in some quicker way.

The end of the story was more slapstick than tragic. While the battle raged, the hastily converted Swiss forgot one day that it was Ramadan and lit a cigarette in the souks of Tunis. If he had been in western clothes this would have earned him no more than a few glares and gross references to his mother's anatomy or father's virility. But the sight of a man in Arab dress flouting the holy fast broke the hungry, thirsty, sullen camel's back. A gang of boys mobbed him, beat him, tore the *gondourah* from his back—and he was thrown in jail for disturbing the peace. Investigation proved—or common opinion guessed (which in Tunisia often amount to the same thing)— that he was not rich at all and had no diamond bracelets or influence in Swiss banks. He left Tunisia abruptly, and Aliya unlocked her door. I hope she reminds her parents of this episode if they ever give her advice again.

Laila never missed a wedding, funeral, or circumcision no matter how remote her connection with the people involved. All these occasions are female affairs—though males play their roles of course, particularly at circumcisions. A Tunisian wedding is especially a feminine monopoly: the guests are all women, the groom is hardly permitted to show his face, and the musicians hired to play are either blind or Jewish. I was therefore surprised when Laila suggested one day that I go with her to a wedding.

"How?" I asked her, "in a *ha'ik*?"

"No, you'd have to take it off inside. Can you play an instrument? You might be a Jew."

"Sorry. I'm not musical."

She was determined to have me go and brooded over the problem for a few days. Then she came to me with a wide eurekan grin. "You have a camera," she said. "You will come to take pictures of the bride. No one will mind," she added condescendingly, "it isn't as if you were an Arab."

I drove her to a large ugly house in a new suburb of Tunis. The bride and the groom were servants, or rather of that breed of half-children, half-slaves to which Laila belonged. But the wedding was first class, and the great ladies of Tunis arrived in taxis and limousines, painted and powdered, in dresses of satin, with jewels and feathers in their hair, all in broad daylight. I saw them arrive, because Laila stationed me in a kind of porter's lodge while she disappeared behind the garden wall. Sharing the lodge was a young Arab, looking dumb and morose, in a clean white *burnous*. From across the garden wall came a shrill concatenation of music and female voices.

Laila came back to me once with lemonade and a plate of cakes. Her eyes were bright with the hysteria with which women affect one another *en masse* and which is so terrifying to men. I imagine Orpheus intruded on the Eurinyes just when this feeling was running high. Laila was laughing at some female joke

63

and made a coarse remark to the boy in the white *burnous*, who smiled wanly. "The bridegroom," she told me with a wink.

The delirium in the garden had reached a frightening pitch when they came for us. The women placed the groom's *burnous* over his head so only his nose showed through the slit, and led him into the arena. Laila came for me. "Be sure to take a picture as they put their hands together. If his is on top, he will be the master. We will see." She laughed and poked me forward as if, being male, I was funny too.

Around the garden at little tables sat the bedizened ladies in the harsh sunlight, fanning themselves to a blaze. I almost expected to see their thumbs turned downward when I appeared. My fellow victim was shoved on the dais in the centre of the garden and took his seat beside the bride. The poor girl did not look human—or rather she resembled a real girl as a Russian Easter egg resembles a real egg. She wore a wide-skirted gown of silver cloth and was encrusted all over with jewels, probably lent for the occasion by her 'family'. Her real face was invisible under a mask of rouge and kohl, and her eyes stared out of pools of shadow with the impassivity of a doll's. The heavy dress made her lean, rather than sit, stiffly across her chair, rigid as a Velasquez infanta. I had heard that Tunisian brides often faint from the weight of their finery and the strain of sitting enthroned through the long ordeal of their weddings. As the groom covered her be-ringed, henna-ed hand with his, I snapped their picture.

I turned to find Laila close behind me. "Look around," she said. "Not at the guests. Look at the musicians."

I followed her glance to the stage at the end of the garden. When the bridegroom had entered, the music stopped but the musicians remained seated at their instruments. In front of them, smiling—at Laila? at me? at the contagious elation of women at weddings?—was the dancer. It was Jamila.

Laila held my arm in a vise and piloted me to the lodge.

Before I could speak she went back to the garden. Soon the groom was led back. He thanked me mechanically for taking the picture and I wished him luck. Then he left.

The music started up again. I cursed Laila for leaving me and Jamila for dancing for a bunch of women. Now I had not been pining for Jamila since Ramadan. There were other distractions abroad. But I had thought of her often and had spoken about her once or twice to Laila. But having waited so patiently this long, I felt I could not wait a minute longer.

A few of the guests came out of the garden and called for their cars. Laila came to my cell.

"The concert will be over in a minute," she said. "You can leave. I won't be home for supper."

"Look here," I said, "stop jumping in and out at me like a Karakouz. What the hell's going on?"

"I *said* the concert will be over in a minute," she said and popped back into the garden.

Just like a puppet show, the music stopped on cue, and in a minute Jamila came round the garden wall. She still wore her dancing dress—it was dark green satin with gold sequins across the breast—but she had lost the aplomb she wore on the stage. She came to the door of my lodge.

"Excuse me. The Negress said there was someone here who would drive me home."

"I'll drive you."

She hesitated. Under the make up, the satin and sequins, she looked diffident as a child.

"I'll change my clothes," she said, and disappeared.

I sat in the lodge feeling the way you do when everything starts to go right, in a painting, or in a dream. When she came out she was in western dress but carried a *ha'ik* folded over her arm. In the car she sat close beside me on the seat, not in the corner the way American girls do. She did not speak at all, except once to ask where we were going.

"I thought we'd drive out to Sidi-bou-Saïd," I said.

She had never been there before, and seemed surprised that I lived in an Arab town. When I stopped the car she unfolded her *ha'ik*, but after glancing up and down the empty street she walked unveiled from the car to my door.

I took her up to the terrace. The sun was going down behind us and Bou Kornine turned violet and pink, like a Beshir painting. Jamila was indifferent to views. She sat with her back to it and munched a fig, sinking her strong teeth through the purple skin and green flesh to the rosy hole in the centre. She had kicked off her shoes at the edge of the mat and sat cross-legged, her feet beneath her. I stretched on a cushion in front of her and, as if I were composing a picture, made her part of the view.

She was not classically beautiful in close-up. Her mouth was too wide and her brow too low. Yet there was something classical in her face—the totally opaque, exterior look of a Greek head of the best period. When she was not expressing an immediate emotion, past and future were erased and her features existed in a pure present. My eyes sank to her firm pointed breasts and the curve of her thighs under the taut skirt. She looked up from the ravished fig and smiled.

"You came to Halfaween at Ramadan and watched me dance. One time you were with a blonde girl—an American."

"That's right. I like to watch you dance. Will you dance for me here?"

"Some time. Then you came to look for me where I lived. You said, 'Jamila is beautiful.' Do you know my real name?"

"Fatma."

"How did you know?"

"I am a *marabout*. Where were you when I came to look for you? Off with some man, I bet."

"No, I——" she faltered. "I had gone home, to my family.

66

I must be very careful. They don't know I do—this." She made a gesture that indicated dancing, parties, and me.

Day dreams should have no past and no future. I put out my hand and drew Jamila back into the present.

After a while she said, "The Negress is not coming home tonight. I will make your supper." She went down into the house. I lay and watched Bou Kornine turn a dark, transparent blue in the fading sky. I felt like a ripe fruit, filled to bursting with the juice of the sun, about to fall from the tree. What went on behind that placid front, I thought. Did she despise all men, and therefore me? Did she look on this as just another professional performance, like dancing for women at a wedding? Or was she actually enjoying it as much as she seemed to be? It was time that *I* returned to the present. The fruit was about to drop.

Jamila came back with some grilled meat, bread, and a bottle of wine. The wine was for me, but she devoured half the meat and bread with frank, carnivorous pleasure. She fed me, as Arab women do. When we had done eating, Jamila went down for some coffee, and after that she brought up my *burnous*.

At four in the morning, we woke to find that the moon had risen, turning the white deck into its own snowy reflection. The *burnous* was drenched with dew.

III. CARTHAGE

PART OF THE PLEASURE OF LIVING IN SIDI-BOU-SAÏD WAS THE knowledge that this had once been a suburb of Carthage, for centuries the greatest city of the western world. The view from my terrace had been the arena of events which had shaped history and still reverberate into modern times. It was the home of Hannibal, Tertullian, and Terence. Cato, Julius Caesar, Hadrian, and Belisarius had seen it. Virgil, St. Augustine, and Apuleius had described it. The scene was part of one's inheritance, living in it like living in a room with portraits of ancestors.

Unfortunately, the most conspicuous object in the foreground of my view was the bombastic cathedral of St. Louis (style Byzantine-Mauresque, circa 1890) that crowns the hill of Byrsa. And modern Carthage itself is a commuters' suburb of *villas coquettes*, pompous colonial mansions and technicolour gardens, built round a congregation of convents, chapels seminaries, and schools, while along the shore sprawls a splendid squalor of mud-coloured outhouses, the summer palace of the last reigning Bey. For Carthage has been destroyed—many times; but she has always bounced back from the graveyard to vivid, wayward life.

Ruins of the past are there of course, buried under the vulgar present or exposed in vacant lots, some half drowned along the beach or hidden under brambles in the outlying fields. Some sites have been tidied up, mosaics swept and relaid, columns and masonry re-erected, for the instruction of students if not of poets. The soil is constantly being sifted and turned, and yields an apparently inexhaustible potpourri of Punic, Roman, Hellenistic, early Christian, oriental, and Byzantine bric-à-brac, of coins, jewellery, kitchen utensils, oil lamps, sarcophagi with their contents, mosaics and inscriptions, and an anatomical survey of marble arms, legs, feet, hands, heads and torsos with noses and penises broken off by time or barbarians. The portable bits have been put in the museum attached to the cathedral on Byrsa or in the Bardo in town, whose collection of mosaics is equal to any in the world. But there is much to see *in situ*, and with a rigorous application of the "selective eye" I liked to take the short drive or the more ambitious walk through the olive groves and into the long perspectives of my view.

Of Punic Carthage little remains, except a few graves and geography itself. The Hill of Byrsa, shorn of its incongruous biretta, may remind us of Elissa, the princess of Tyre who became Dido 'the fugitive', a true Semite who won the hill from the natives by a Levantine trick—fit beginning for the world's greatest commercial empire. The view from Byrsa is almost as fine as that from Sidi-bou-Saïd, and Elissa, if she existed, must have been familiar with the shapes of Cap Bon and Bou Kornine, whether or not she saw them last with dying, love-forsaken eyes. The older legends relate that she killed herself for politics, not love, because she refused to marry a native prince as her followers desired.

"Harsh and gloomy, docile to their rulers, hard to their subjects, turning to extremes of cowardice in fear and savagery in anger"; thus Plutarch describes the Carthaginians. "Punic faith" was a Roman byword for treachery, and crucifixion, often practiced on their own unsuccessful generals, was among their inventions. So far the enemies of Carthage. But there is proof among the ruins of the worst the Romans said. In a quiet residential street of modern Carthage is a Punic cemetery from which a whiff of horror seeps across the centuries. The small lot has yielded thousands of clay pots, empty now, but once the repository of the ashes of children. For the Carthaginians practised the unaimiable rite of child sacrifice. Their god Baal demanded the first born male of every family, and in times of trouble He could be propitiated only by holocausts of boys of noble blood who were consumed alive in His fiery arms. Some pots are bigger than others; these, the smiling guardian of the site explains, contained the charred bones of older children whose impious parents evaded the sacrifice at birth but were found out or repented themselves under some later catastrophe.

There is another memento of Punic Carthage that is more attractive. Looking down from Byrsa you can see two ponds side by side on the edge of the bay. They are outlines of the ancient port. Silted with time and partly filled in for later purposes, they gaze serenely at the sky, unruffled now by the tides of commerce or war. You can walk round them as you might a duck pond and ponder how they once held empire over half the known world, sending ships as far as Britain and down the coast of Africa to Senegal. Out of these harbours at some point in their careers sailed the two most famous of Carthaginians, heroes of universal significance, Hamilcar Barca and his son Hannibal. They each in turn pitted themselves against the rising might of Rome, in Sicily, Spain, Italy, and North Africa, with considerable skill and deadly hatred; and if their luck had held, we might now be speaking remnants of a semitic language and living under a pattern of Punic law. But Hannibal was at last beaten on his own ground and, pursued by the Romans through the courts of the East, drank a cup of poison and died.

Elissa and Hannibal: the history of Punic Carthage began and ended with suicide, just as the sacrifice of her own infants was a ritual form of suicide. Shorn of her empire and constrained to keep the peace, Carthage was provoked into an attack on an

Carthage—Basilica of St. Cyprian

African ally of Rome. The Romans immediately mobilised and sent word to the city: Carthage must be destroyed. The Punic deputies returning with this decree were stoned to death by the people. The seige lasted three years for the defenders fought with the force of despair. When the walls were finally pierced by assault, the fighting advanced house by house and street by street. The Romans burnt the town as they went. Byrsa fell on the seventh day and the great temple was set on fire, consuming hundreds in a final holocaust. The city burned for seventeen days. The survivors, fifty thousand of a population that had numbered 700,000, were sold into slavery. The charred ruins were razed to the ground, the soil sown with salt, and a curse pronounced over the site. The city of Carthage had vanished from the earth.

One of my favourite excursions into the past lay among the olive groves between Sidi-bou-Saïd and Carthage, among the hills of La Malga. Shepherds lived in the ancient cisterns, and the ruins here were largely unedited, their original purpose as cryptic as an undeciphered language. It must have been another suburb, for there are several rows of Roman villas—nothing now but an architect's print laid out in white and black mosaics —overlooking the bay. I liked to take a shaker of martinis and sit in a late Roman atrium and watch the sun fade on the mountains across the bay. Once I took Jamila with me.

Like most Tunisians she had never heard of Dido and Aeneas. So I told her Virgil's story.

"Were they Arabs?" she wanted to know.

"She was, sort of—from Syria. He was an Italian." It seemed the simplest version of their antecedents.

Arabs are good listeners. Jamila laughed at Dido's trick with the bull's hide strips. She approved the episode of the hunting party and the love making in the cave. Then I told her how Dido broke her vow of widowhood by asking Aeneas to marry her.

"Did he?" she asked hopefully.

"No," I confessed. "He left her."

"Why? Was he in love with someone else?" (Jamila loved sad movies and the Arabic versions of *True Confessions*.)

"No. There was some business he had to attend to in Rome." Reluctantly, I recounted how he had sneaked off in the night, how Dido saw the ships sailing out of the bay, and how she had built a fire of his gifts and stabbed herself.

Jamila stared silently out to where his ships had disappeared north of Cap Bon. Then, "Did he ever know?"

"Her ghost came to him in a dream. He was very sorry."

Jamila got up from the ground. "I don't think she was an Arab," she said.

"Why? Don't Arab women kill themselves for love?"

"Lord no!" she laughed down at me. "They would kill the man that left them first."

Virgil's story is a Roman novelette, well suited to martinis, a pretty girl, and late Roman ruins. But whence came these villas, cisterns, temples, fora, theatres, baths, arenas—the whole extraordinary elaboration of a Hellenistic metropolis? Carthage had been destroyed, but in less than a generation—and not without the disapprobation of those who believe in curses—a colony of Roman veterans had been planted on the spot. With that superb vitality that seemed to spring from the site, Carthage was soon the leading city of Africa once more, second only to Rome in the west. Judging from what remains, it must have been a rich, grandiose, cultivated, pleasure-loving, vulgar, and extremely comfortable place.

The most impressive monument unearthed so far is not a temple or a court of law, but the baths of Antonin. An edifice of Caracallan grandeur, it stood three storeys high and covered several acres along the shore. The plumbing, now surgically exposed, was downright American in complexity, with pipes for hot and cold, fresh and salt water, and huge blackened furnaces in the basement. A capital of frosty Carrara marble, four tons of intricately carved figures and foliage, was hurled by some cataclysm through the upper floors to the basement where it lies like a petrified piece of a gargantuan wedding cake. The marble counterpart of all the steamy sensuality this served can be seen in a colony of statues that have survived, among them several naked, effeminate Apollos with long hair and Elvis Presley hips, who might illustrate Shakespeare's lines:

> And for a woman wert thou first created,
> Till Nature as she wrought thee fell adoting,
> And by addition me of thee defeated,
> By adding one thing—to my purpose nothing.

Roman Carthage was noted for its painted male harlots.

Apuleius, author of that ancestor of the novel *The Golden Ass*, lived here. His description of the rogues and witches, whores, innkeepers, highway robbers, Cupid and Psyche, and the adepts of Osiris must have been drawn from the facts and fancies of second century Carthage. One story he tells is about a convicted murderess who was sentenced to public outrage by the Ass before being devoured by wild beasts. The amphitheatre where such foul punishments were performed still stands. I sometimes climbed the bowl of seats—more than knocked about, the stones seem to have decayed in their sockets, like a mouthful of carious teeth—and wonder what kind of people they were who looked on torture and death as a day's entertainment. What was it like to look down from this gallery into that arena and see the fangs puncture the skin, the arm torn from the socket, the short sword plunged into the groin, and pain and terror glaze the victim's eye? Did the ordinary mason or clerk who occupied these highest and cheapest seats take home some spiritual gain, a quickened awareness of the sweetness of life, the meaning of death?

Cicero thought so: he found the games an "incomparable training to make the spectator despise suffering and death." St. Augustine seems to me nearer the mark when he tells of a friend who was taken to a gladiatorial show against his will. He was determined not to look, but a shout from· the crowd roused his curiosity and involuntarily opening his eyes, he "was stricken with a deeper wound in his soul than the other, whom he desired to behold, was in his body. . . . For so soon as he saw that blood, he therewith drank down savageness; nor turned away, but fixed his eye, drinking in frenzy unawares, and was delighted with that guilty fight, and intoxicated with the bloody pastime."

Among those who died here were two of the most attractive saints in the Christian calendar, Perpetua, a young patrician, and Felicity, a slave, who were arrested as Christians and sentenced to be torn to pieces for the amusement of the public and the safety of the state. Perpetua's father begged her to recant but she refused. Felicity was eight months' pregnant and feared that her condition might prevent her dying with her companion, but she was delivered three days before the games. Perpetua's son was taken from her just before the holiday; "God granted that he no longer asked for my breast," she wrote in her journal, "and that I was not tormented by my milk." The two young mothers were wrapped in a net and delivered to the goring of a wild cow. They seemed indifferent to pain and drew their torn garments about them for the sake of modesty. When the animal was driven off for the death blow, Perpetua bound her dishevelled hair to show that she was not in mourning at her moment of glory. Their graves have been found in a corner of Carthage, and a rose has been given their names.

Tertullian, that early Christian fire-eater, was another Carthaginian. "Crucify, torture, condemn, crush us beneath your feet," he dared the authorities; "the more you mow us

down the more we spring up; the blood of Christians is seed."
Tertullian himself was never a martyr, though it must have
been a great temptation to make him one. Born a pagan and
classically educated, he turned savagely against his and the
world's past. He was a good hater: tracts against pagans, Jews,
heretics, the government, carnality, the theatre, and dyed hair
poured from his pen. In the end the Church branded him a
heretic himself because he insisted on personal conscience and
continuing revelation. He was in fact an early Protestant, an
African Savonarola or John Knox, come several centuries too
soon.

One of the pleasantest excursions between my house and
Byrsa led along the coast to a small plateau where seven grassy
aisles ran between rows of shorn-off columns to the edge of a
cliff that slices abruptly into the bay. This was the basilica of St.
Cyprian, bishop and patron of Carthage, whose tolerant,
civilised personality seems part of the attraction of the place.
Also born a pagan, into a rich Carthaginian family, he was converted to Christianity in middle age. He immediately went
into hiding for fourteen months to avoid persecution; but for
ten years thereafter he was a wise and understanding shepherd
to his flock. Where Tertullian was tart and uncompromising,
Cyprian was urbane and conciliatory. He showed that one can
believe and still not wish to meet a horrible death. In the end
everything came his way, including martyrdom and canonisa-
tion. But one feels he had to overcome a real human dread to
face the executioner.

Carthage is full of the dead fruit of official Christianity—
churches, baptismal fonts, votive reliefs, gravestones—all as
deplorable in their way as the 1890 cathedral. The new religious fervour did nothing to revive the deterioration of the
classic style—which should make us leery of equating artistic
and spiritual mediocrity. The monuments of North African
Christianity are of the mind, and the greatest of them were

built by a Numidian who came to Carthage as a schoolboy in the year 370 from Bône in Algeria.

There is no particular spot in Carthage associated with St. Augustine, though he must have known every street and quarter, from the lowest to the most rarified, in his famous, self-revealed career from intellectual adventurer to father of the Church. We may find his early portrait as Manichæan and *bon vivant* more attractive; but in his later role he had a powerful effect on the medieval mind almost impossible to exaggerate. He helped develop monasticism and a strong papacy; emphasised original sin and had a close brush with predestination; "The authority of the scriptures," he declared, "is higher than all the efforts of the human intelligence." Though he walked among the sunlit columns and classic, humanist décor of Carthage, Augustine's mind already inhabited the soaring, shadowy nave of a Gothic cathedral.

Carthage herself was about to undergo two more metamorphoses, perhaps the oddest in her protean career. The next two centuries were to produce, first a Vandal, then a Byzantine Carthage.

The names of certain peoples have become common names describing a moral quality or recurrent type of man. Spartan, Sybarite, Tartar, Hottentot, Prussian, and Scot are now epithets, their rich and no doubt contradictory humanity boiled down to a single sharp impression, like a colour or a fault. Vandal and Byzantine are such labels, denoting two extremes of mankind in society—the destroyer and the preserver, the barbarous yahoo who defaces what he cannot comprehend, and the refined pedagogue who indexes what he cannot create. The symbols are more real than the historic facts, as shown by their survival. A war between Byzantines and Vandals can hardly be imagined but in terms of ritual enacted with the solemnity of high mass, a confrontation of hieratic figures worked in mosaic on a gold ground. Such a war took place in Carthage.

The Vandals crossed from Spain into Africa in 420—
150,000 men, women, and children, led by their lame and
ferocious chief, Gaeseric. It took them ten years to subdue the
walled cities. When Carthage finally fell, Gaeseric did not
destroy it. He put it to the customary pillage, enslaved the
Roman nobles and priests, and converted the churches to
Arianism, a Christian heresy the Vandals had picked up in their
travels. Gaeseric resoundingly proclaimed himself Rex Vandalorum et Alanorum of Carthage and used the city as a base
for a very successful career of piracy.

Far from 'vandalising' Carthage, the Vandals enriched it
with the spoils of Sicily, Greece, and Rome. Among the loot
they brought back from a successful raid on Rome were the
imperial insignia, the gilded roof of the Temple of Jupiter, and
the vessels from the Temple in Jerusalem. Gaeseric also brought
back as captives the empress Eudoxia and her two daughters,
one of whom he married to his son and heir, thus acquiring
respectability in the family. The Vandals destroyed a Byzantine fleet off Cap Bon by sending blazing boats among them,
and halted a Roman punitive expedition from Spain by
scorching the earth and poisoning the wells of Mauretania. The
Byzantine emperor was at last forced to recognise a new
Carthaginian empire stretching from the Balearic islands to
Tripolitania. Gaeseric died ripe in age, warmed by memories of
rapine, slaughter, and conquest.

His successors were true to the tradition of the heirs of self-
made men. Living in the urbane decor of Carthage or amid the
abundance of a Roman farm, the Baltic terror grew civilised in
one generation and decadent in two. They dressed in soft garments and the imperial trappings of Rome; polished Latin
replaced the harsh gutturals of the North. In less than a century
the fatal lure of the south for the German soul had transformed
the *herrenvolk* into *fin-de-siècle* exquisites.

And now the other half of the mosaic, the antiphony of the

Mass. An African bishop fleeing from Vandal rule appeared at the Byzantine court and told the Emperor Justinian of a dream he had had that God Himself would lead the Byzantines to victory in Carthage. There were many practical arguments against the expedition (including the memory of those fire ships off Cap Bon) but the bishop's dream prevailed. The Emperor sent his general, Belisarius, to land on the coast south of Carthage and engage the Vandals. He had trouble finding them at first and marched almost unopposed on Carthage. After two engagements near the city, the Vandal king fled up a mountain in Algeria, from which he descended only on Belisarius' promise of personal safety, to be led in triumph to Byzantium. Justinian assumed the titles of Vandalorum and Africanus, and had portrayed in a mosaic such as we have imagined, the Vandal king's obeisance to himself and his consort Theodora.

The Byzantine 'Restoration' lasted less than a century. It was on the defensive, first against the Berber tribes who menaced the interior, then against its own mutinous troops and officials. Carthage itself grew listless, the famous, apparently inexhaustable vitality sapped by a century of wars, heresies, and Byzantine administration. Though sustained by the imperial fleet, the city could not halt the disintegration of the provinces. Then a new peril rode out of the sands of Libya—raiders who struck, defeated both Byzantines and Berbers, and withdrew into the desert. They were Arabs, forerunners of the Moslem conquest that was to change the very climate and spirit of North Africa and reduce Carthage to the ruins we see today.

The Arabs did worse than destroy Carthage : they ignored it. Moslem power attached itself to other places, and Carthage was reduced to a storehouse and quarry of prefabricated architecture, stone, and lime for the new centres. Europeans came also and took away such souvenirs as the columns for the cathedral of Pisa, and early consuls did a brisk trade in antiquities for the museums at home. The Arabs and Turks did not care, and the bedouin who lived in the cisterns and grazed their flocks on the floors of temples and basilicas must have looked in astonishment at the backbreaking labour of sailors from the 19th-century British man-o'-war that stood alongside and loaded up with great chunks of the baths of Antonin.

History visited Carthage once more in the forlorn little episode that foreshadowed French interference in North Africa. King Louis IX stopped here in 1270 en route to a crusade in the Holy Land. He camped among the ruins, and the ladies in his train are said to have enjoyed the fancy that their tents were pitched in the palace of Queen Dido. This medieval picnic was cut short by Louis' death from the plague. There is a story current in Tunisia that he did not really die, but converted to Islam, moved from Byrsa to the neighbouring hill and became a Moslem saint, in fact, Sidi-bou-Saïd. In any case, a French consul acquired Byrsa from the Bey of Tunis in the 19th century and erected a tomb for the royal saint. From this seed sprang the whole proliferation of religious establishments that flowered in the Byzantine-Moorish cathedral, as well as the Church's long husbandry that preceded and accompanied France's self-styled *mission civilisatrice* in Barbary.

History, like the Moslems, moved elsewhere, leaving the marks and deposits of its successsive waves in the soil like those impressions of a scallop shell or seaweed we find in rocks far inland. One recent flood has washed up a bit of flotsam of modern history. The bodies of the American dead of World War II in North Africa have been gathered in a permanent cemetery in Carthage. They lie under ordered ranks of marble crosses and stars on a lawn of clipped and watered grass, not far from a burial ground of early Christians. The green and white field was startling but refreshing amid the tawny hills and grey olive trees, and I liked to think that this relic of our own catastrophes will take its place in some future Carthage among the alluvium of the ages.

IV. AROUND THE BAY

AN ELECTRIC TRAIN USED TO START IN THE MIDDLE OF TUNIS and run straight across the lake. This feat was accomplished by means of a narrow causeway resting on the shallow bottom and raising the tracks just a few feet above the water. It was a pleasant trip, full of incongruities. Pink flamingo stood knee-deep in the shallows feeding on goodness knows what filth from the bottom and gazing unamazed at the suburban commuters. Arab fishermen, their clothes rolled up to the waist, cast nets a few yards from the track. Occasionally you saw a dolphin rollicking its way up the channel like a sailor nearing port. And ocean-going ships came within hailing distance of the little white-painted railway cars. This engaging journey has now been superseded by an efficient bus service, faster and more comfortable, but lacking a certain sense of adventure.

The train stopped first at La Goulette. Pressed between the lake and the bay, the town is a string of dilapidated houses and run-down squares, with an untidy strip of beach, the cheap attractions of a summer resort and expensive furnishings of a yacht harbour, and on the business side a fishing fleet and a modern port. But La Goulette shows traces of better, if grimmer, days. The grey sixteenth-century fortress frowns down upon the seedy, frivolous present. La Goulette was not only the principal outwork of Tunis, but also a pirate lair and *bagnio* for Christian captives awaiting sale or ransom who at one time numbered ten thousand in the entire Beylic. In 1535 the forces of the Emperor Charles V took La Goulette by assault; the defendants were led by a gentleman known to history as Sinan the Jew; the released captives joined the Emperor's troops in a thorough sack of Tunis. After Lepanto, Don Juan of Austria improved the fortifications, but the Turks recaptured it the following year and again put Tunis to the sack. Cervantes fought among the Emperor's troops at La Goulette, and St. Vincent de Paul was brought here after having been captured at sea and sold in the slave-market of Tunis. His purchaser was a renegade Frenchman whom the saint reconverted and persuaded to return to France with him. Less fortunate captives, if not ransomed, were chained to the oars of a Turkish galley or disappeared into the harems of the East. Many, however, 'took the turban' and became pirates themselves. Their descendants undoubtedly live in La Goulette today.

La Goulette is part of what might be called Levantine Tunisia, one of those conglomerations of races that teem in Mediterranean ports from Marseilles to Beirut. Sicilians, Corsicans, Maltese, Spaniards, Greeks, and Jews, they add a rich flavour of garlic and sweat and the spice of spontaneity to the Tunisian *bouillabaisse*. Italians once outnumbered the French in Tunisia and had their own schools, newspapers, aristocracy, and professional class. But after the war, the French deported the rich and influential and confiscated their property; only the Sicilian proletariat was left. Every spring they come out *en masse* in a religious procession that flows through the streets of La Goulette like a tide, bearing a statue of the Virgin and chanting orisons to the goddess of the sea. Every summer a Spanish circus with a family air and nothing fiercer than some trained dogs and cats used to play here. The amusement piers extended Ramadan nights throughout the season. And on hot summer evenings it is the fashion to come and eat Jewish food.

On these evenings, the main street is turned into one long

dining-room served by many kitchens. The sidewalks disappear under an underbrush of tables, and the dark—which all Mediterraneans hate—is defeated by strings of naked bulbs. The waiters rush from table to table, and you are lucky to get clean linen. The menus are written up on blackboards outside each kitchen. The food is fishy—*loup de mer*, sea urchins, baby octopus; or earthy—one speciality is a stew of bulls' balls. You wash this down with *boukha*, a fiery aquavit made of figs. The impact of one of these meals has been known to make a Western stomach go into reverse.

Another gustatory attraction of La Goulette is the parade of young Jewesses. Tunisian Jewish girls are among the prettiest in the world, with milky skins, eyes like melted topazes or sapphires, and figures agreeably *embonpoint*. Years ago they used to be kept in darkened rooms to whiten the skin and forcibly fed like penned pullets to achieve the desired figure. The methods have changed, but they still give careful attention to their beauty care. They dress in the latest Paris styles, with an oriental opulence of brocade and watered silk. The young Moslem and Christian bloods are very partial to them, and during the war the allied soldiers were bowled over. They walk in the streets of La Goulette on summer evenings, in small animated groups of three or four, unapproachable but deliciously on display.

The Jews do their part to enrich the Tunisian racial stew. Numbering less than eighty thousand, they nevertheless claim great diversity of origin. Some boast descent from refugees fleeing the destruction of Jerusalem by Nebuchadrezzar and to be settled in Tunisia for 2,500 years. Others, perhaps the majority, are thought to be converted Berbers, hence racially identical with many so-called Arabs. Then there are Jews of Livorno, 'Leghorns' whose ancestors came from Spain and Italy during the past four hundred years. And the upheavals of the 20th century have brought new arrivals from France,

Germany, and central Europe. They vary in physical type as in origin. The rarest is the gingery Slav or the Hittite profile of *Judenhetze* caricature. The most distinctive type is white-skinned with dark crinkly hair and somewhat unformed, childish features; it can be ravishing in the females, though a bit insipid in the males.

Under the absolute rule of the Beys, the Jews endured the precarious status of all minorities. As late as the mid-nineteenth century a British consul reported the punishment of a Moslem woman and Jewish man caught in adultery. The woman was smothered in the mud of the Lake; the Jew had boiling oil poured down his throat, and his severed head was afterwards used as a football in the streets. We may think that the woman suffered as much as the man, but the British consul pointed out that the posthumous outrage would not have been inflicted on a Moslem head. He thought the Bey's subjects should have a constitution; but the Bey's subjects—at least the Moslem majority—rioted at the suggestion.

In the long sleep of the Turkish centuries, Judaism in Tunisia lagged behind the slow but progressive way of the rest of the world. Polygamy, abolished by European Jewry some thousand years ago, was permitted, though rarely practised among Tunisian Jews, until it became illegal for all Tunisian citizens in 1956. Unmarried Jewesses, no matter what their age, remained legally minor and under the authority of their father or elder brothers. In order to marry, a Jewish girl had to pay for a husband, and the price of a really good catch was high. I knew a family of five pretty and accomplished daughters who were turning into old maids while their father tried to raise the money to get them suitable husbands. Perhaps that is why the girls make themselves so attractive—to knock a little off the price.

For the most part Tunisian Jews are cheerfully assimilative. Arabic is their mother tongue, and many family names are shared by Jews and Moslem alike. Under the Turks, they were made to wear distinctive dress; even today some of the older women walk through the streets of La Goulette or Tunis in loose white trousers and *ha'iks* over their shoulders like shawls. But in the cities where the great majority live, young Jews now strive to look and sound as European as possible. French has become their first language, and they give their children names like René, Francine, or Colette. The young men served in the French Army. Many acquired French nationality and have moved to France. A friend of mine whose father was a proud *ancien combattant* tells of his own circumcision, his father dressed in uniform and medals, while the band played '*La Marseillaise*'. In the last days of the Protectorate, many Tunisian Jews supported the Arabs' demand for reforms; since independence there has always been a Jewish minister in the cabinet. Neither the Arabs nor the Jews of Tunisia are very excited over Israel. Those that have gone there are the very religious Jews who remember Nebuchadrezzar. A few want to emigrate to Europe or the United States. Most intend to stay where they are.

The train continued round the rim of the lake, through a belt of commuters' dormitories that merge into each other without distinction. They are new towns, given 'historic' names like Amilcar and Salammbô, all within the precincts of ancient Carthage but totally lacking any *genius loci*. One of them, if not a place, was the home of a woman who was at least a person.

Mrs. Preston could have been taken for no one but herself. I first saw her at a reception given by the American Consulate for a visiting Navy ship. Mrs. Preston enjoyed such affairs to the full, surrounded by white-clad officers who were clearly enjoying themselves too—a large woman in flowered chiffon and a wide-brimmed hat, with an aura of scandal about her like a heady perfume. The current scandal in Mrs. Preston's life was that she was married to a Moslem who already had a wife and several children. "My husband is so sweet to me," she would say disarmingly, "that I do what I can for his other wife and children." Mrs. Preston was wealthy and lived in her own house in the European quarter. The husband, a bath-house attendant, kept his other wife and their children in a house in the Arab quarter near the baths that Mrs. Preston had bought for him.

Roxane took me to call the first time. Mrs. Preston received us in a jade green dressing-gown, among the advanced decor of another age. The room was cluttered with a stuffed peacock, a profusion of Spanish shawls, dressmakers' dummies in brilliant outmoded gowns, and glass cabinets crammed with mementoes of a varied life.

Mrs. Preston was as frank about the past as the present. "When I lived with Z," she would say, naming one of the nearly great painters of the recent past. Or, "X adored my thighs." She took us to the studio, stacked high with her own indifferent painting. The famous portrait of her by Z. glowered from an easel as if it had just been done: the face of a diabolic madonna lit by some distant conflagration. The picture by X was of a different school. It was larger than life and dominated the room by audacity. It was a nude, half standing, half sitting in a woodland glade, holding a flower to the lips and stretching one leg to dabble a dimpled toe in a purling stream. The blonde hair was piled high in the fashion of the day, with a few ringlets straying about the sweet, empty face. The breasts peeped out like rosebuds from behind the bent arm, and the hips and thighs seemed made of something pink and edible like strawberry whipped cream.

During tea we talked of art and then religion. "I am a Moslem," Mrs. Preston said, "for otherwise I would be under French laws and my marriage would be bigamous. Of course I don't believe in God. Do you?" she asked Roxane.

I knew that Roxane did, at least when she was in Italy.

"Well, yes, I think I do," Roxane said as if confessing to an amiable weakness. "When one is in a beautiful church, like St. Peter's or——"

"Museums!" Mrs. Preston interjected. "Very beautiful no doubt, but dead museums." She put the daring old-fashioned question to me.

"I'm not sure," I said. "At least I don't think I like Him very much."

"Now, that's interesting. Does that mean you don't like life? That would be a pity. Have you never been in love?" Something like beauty flashed in and out of her ageing face.

We stayed an hour but the husband did not appear. We were disappointed.

Some months later Roxane noticed that Mrs. Preston had missed a Navy party and telephoned her. She was ill and asked us to call. This time she received us in bed, in a billowy disarray of linen that I thought only existed in eighteenth century-boudoir prints. But the silken turbulence was real, and so was Mrs. Preston's distress. Her face was as white and puffy as the bed clothes.

"Look at me!" she greeted us, throwing off the covers to show her swollen legs. "Look at those sausages!" Her voice trembled with horror and she began to weep.

I left Roxane with her and went to find a servant to ask about the medical arrangements.

Downstairs I found a man sitting in the kitchen and asked him abruptly: "Who is looking after Mrs. Preston?"

"I am, Monsieur," he said sorrowfully. "I am her husband."

"I am sorry, Monsieur," I said. "Your wife is very ill. Has she seen a doctor?"

"The best I could find," he answered and named one well known.

"What does he say?"

The husband turned his face away and did not reply.

In the car going back to Tunis I noticed that Roxane's mascara had run on to her cheek.

Most funerals are depressing not because they are sad—for sorrow is not depressing—but because they are artificial. They seem to have nothing to do with the person being buried. Mrs. Preston's funeral was personal and not depressing at all; I am sure it had been arranged by herself. Her husband telephoned to give us the time and place. "She would like you and your lady to come," he said, as if he were inviting us to a party.

The funeral was held from Mrs. Preston's house. A group of men of all nationalities stood about in the garden. Her husband, in a new pink *gondourah* and raspberry *tarbush*, met us at the door. In the studio, draped with a black and rose Spanish shawl, was the coffin. It lay directly under the girl with the adorable thighs, dipping her toe in the perpetual stream and sniffing the unfading flower. Standing in the room, red-eyed with weeping, were several Arab women in the graceful old-fashioned *foutah*. Mrs. Preston's husband introduced them to us as his other wife and daughters. A grown son, whose looks showed what must have attracted Mrs. Preston to the father, stood beside him.

There was no ceremony. Eight of the men from the garden came in and hoisted the coffin to their shoulders. We followed them out and joined the long cortège that walked through the streets to the cemetery. The Arab women stayed behind, and except for Roxane the procession was entirely male—perhaps, I thought, they had all loved Mrs. Preston and in some way made life sweet for her.

At the grave there was neither prayer nor eulogy. The only sounds were the shuffling of the lovers' feet and the creak of the ropes as the coffin was lowered into the ground. As it settled in the earth, there was a deep involuntary sob from Mrs. Preston's husband.

. . . . .

The train ran on through Carthage and past the foot of Sidi-bou-Saïd to La Marsa, a courtly town, the ancient seat of the Beys. Fine old palaces stand in vacant gardens or along the sea front, with a blind, lofty look and an attractive air of having come down in the world. Aged eunuchs still appear in the streets, though more and more rarely, portly smooth-faced men who walk with an air of offended dignity. They were once important officials in the Bey's household and live on as reminders of how rapidly the past becomes obsolete. The Bey's dwarfs were also a frequent sight in the cafés of La Marsa. In the reign of the last Bey they were still useful members of court, taking the place of satirical magazines and television. One of them was said to watch the Bey's audiences through a peephole and later do take-offs of the French officials who came to give the Bey his orders. The Bey's dwarfs were treated with amused respect by the townspeople of La Marsa, who were not too embarrassed to laugh at nature's little jokes.

The brightest bit of colour in La Marsa were the men and officers of the Beylical guard. Their uniforms consisted of cherry red trousers, braided blue bolero jackets, and garnet *chechias* decorated with long black tassels. In true Graustarkian tradition, there were almost as many generals as privates. The privates guarded the Bey's palaces and sometimes the French Residency General, and marched to the sinuous Turkish music of the Beylical band—which made even the Marseillaise sound like a belly dance. There was a saying that a man entered the Guards an ass and came out a mule. This diverting relic has now disappeared into the efficient, khaki-clad Tunisian Army.

All this was part of Turkish Tunisia, another of the fossilised societies that survive in the hospitable climate of Barbary. The Beys were not Arabs, but of Greek or Turkish descent, probably from Crete. The founder of the line, Sidi Hassine, a Captain of Cavalry, seized power in Tunis in 1705. He and his successors ruled by *firman* of the Sublime Porte, but they were absolute sovereigns in their own country. The succession went not from father to son, but to the eldest male descendant of Sidi Hassine, an arrangement that was supposed to eliminate the Turkish custom of brother poisoning brother. Turkish fashion, the Beys imported their officials, favourites, and slaves from Circassia, the Balkans, Italy, and Greece. Piracy was their principal source of revenue.

In the throne room of the Bardo Palace in Tunis hang the portraits of most of this crew. One of them shows a dark-bearded man in a frock coat, with a hurt look in his eyes and a sensual underlip that might easily quiver. He was a pre-Protectorate Bey, but his tastes and habits are still current gossip. His favourite was Ali, a Circassian slave boy of remarkable beauty and intelligence, who began his career as a barber and rose through the Bey's bed to the office of prime minister. One of his jobs, after he had outgrown the role himself, was to procure other playmates for his master. Ali was ruthless in his requisitions: it is said that no Tunisian family, no matter how rich or powerful, was safe; sons were seized from their fathers in the street; and parents took to sending their likely offspring into hiding in the country, or even abroad. The Bey's taste and discrimination became legendary. He had con-constructed a saddle of wax on which his partners were first placed and then abruptly lifted for depilation. He instituted a decoration called the Order of Little Ali which he bestowed on those boys who could perform a sexual feat introduced by his original favourite. Ali himself became an insatiable lover of women, and the hard-pressed parents of Tunisia had to hide their daughters as well from his requisitions.

This ancient but still living gossip was retailed to me by a Tunisian whose family had been members of the court for generations.

"Was this Bey married?" I asked. "Did he have any children?"

"Of course," my informant replied: "he had a *private* life as well."

Under the Protectorate, Republican France was obliged by treaty to preserve the autocratic prerogatives of the Bey in perpetuity. In theory the reigning Bey had power of life and death over his subjects; in practice, modern Beys were lenient and unobtrusive, their power felt only within the Hassinite family. A Beylical jail existed, reserved for peccant princes; but it was always empty like the tender-hearted theologian's hell and stood as a warning. No prince was allowed to work. Few of them were educated. They could not travel without permission of the sovereign—and the other branches of the family were usually on bad terms with the sovereign. Not surprisingly, they were bored and sometimes dangerous. They drove expensive automobiles through the streets of La Marsa with equal contempt for the laws of the land and the laws of chance. Some of them had Faroukian reputations for sexual athleticism. One or two were notorious smokers of hashish. There were unsolved rumours of attempted poisoning within the family, and the sons of the last reigning Bey were popularly believed to have been involved in chicanery and intrigue. My friends of Sidi-bou-Saïd were notable exceptions to this unsavouriness.

La Marsa remains in my memory for another reason: it was there that Jamila introduced me to *kif. Kif*—the word means pleasure—is a drug that I have heard variously identified as marihuana or hashish. Its use was an old-fashioned vice in Tunisia, the prerogative of elderly gentlemen who sat in the corners of the native coffee houses silently puffing on long-stemmed pipes.

Jamila usually avoided public places of the traditional Arab kind, explaining that she did not want to be seen by anyone who knew her or her family. However she made an exception for the café in La Marsa, as she wanted me to try *kif*. "It is like your wine," she explained, "but for Moslems, much better."

She led me through the dense souks of La Marsa one night as if she were following a scent. At last we came to the right place: a coffee house, square and vaulted, without furniture but divided into a number of low platforms covered with mats on which a few customers sat cross-legged, with coffee or tea and their pipes on a tray beside them. We walked through the troughs between the platforms to a deep niche, the ledge of which was also above floor level, where we sat in dark privacy. The proprietor who took our order was an emaciated wisp of a man, his eyes dull and tongue thickened with addiction to his wares. Jamila ordered glasses of tea and a pipe.

I wish I could report some sensational enlargement of experience from *kif*. It is said to require long apprenticeship to reveal its charm. After two pipes I began to feel sick. Jamila was disappointed and thought it was my fault. She got cross; I had a headache; and that night we quarrelled.

It was not the first time. Jamila was an enchanting companion, with a robust sensuality, an alert unspoiled mind, and the innocent depravity of an animal or a child. She enjoyed posing for me, and I liked painting her firm tawny body whose contours and colouring reminded me of the low-lying Tunisian hills. One day I was intent on pursuing this metaphor when I felt a blow on the back of my head and was showered with a spate of abuse. Absent-mindedly I had painted in some dark vegetation the way it grows in the fold of a Tunisian valley. This was insulting: Jamila, like all self-respecting Tunisian women, shaved. I do not refer to this kind of quarrel, which is born of the moment and passes with it. But Jamila insisted on burdening the present, not only with a past, but with a future.

She referred frequently to the marriage of the American Army officer and the belly dancer which had surprised all of Tunis during the War. This couple still lived in Tunis and were in fact an unusually happy and devoted pair. Their story was enshrined among the romantic legends of Jamila's world, part of the folklore of her profession. I thought the story of Dido and Aeneas was a more universal expression of such encounters. Our quarrel the night of the *kif* was a trivial, ignoble squabble, but it had roots in both the future and the past.

On the far western lip of the bay lies the cape of Farina. No railway runs this far, only a rough road that passes over several narrow, unstable bridges. The modern world seems to have stopped somewhere along this road; when you cross the last bridge it is like entering the Barbary coast of two or three centuries ago.

There are two towns on the cape. One branch of the road ends in Raf-Raf, in a small but surprisingly elegant square. I always had the feeling that a play was about to begin in that square: a few stately house fronts for backdrop, some narrow alleys for entrance and exit, a brilliant awning stretched over a market of gaudy wares, and always a chorus of expectant, picturesque natives. I am tempted to say that the people of Raf-Raf looked like riff-raff; at any rate they were decidedly raffish. The men were unshaven, often one-eyed from trachoma, and encased in *jebbahs*, a thick, foetal garment that made them look hunch-backed and frequently one-armed. The women were swathed in barbaric purple and red. There were children everywhere, the boys deformed like their fathers, the little girls unveiled with huge liquid eyes in dwindling features, gold hoops in their ears, and henna-stained hands. The pirate faces regarded them tenderly, with the Arab's adoration of children.

There was no tenderness in the hard stares they gave to visitors. Whatever drama was about to begin, I felt that our role in it might call for walking the plank or sitting on the point of a sword in that playful Turkish game known as *hazzouk*. Normally no Arab can resist giving advice on how to manœuvre an automobile, but these watched unsmiling and unhelpful as we backed clumsily, trying to avoid children and donkeys, to turn back on the road we had come.

Raf-Raf faces the sea with a gambler's bravado. Porto Farina is a prudent town like Tunis, and shelters behind a shallow, marshy lagoon. It was converted to a naval base by the Dey of Algiers in the 17th century and keeps the formal outline and handsome martial aspect of its origin. The road runs under fortifications of dark reddish stone and through a series of square courtyards. Dense, rough-coated cypress trees stand under the walls, and the windows are high, small, and barred, it looks like a prison, and in fact it has been so used in modern times. The natives live like wardens and turnkeys in this grim magnificence. The state prisoners repair the 17th century masonry of the Dey's port and shovel the salt which forms in accretions on the edge of the lagoon. If the looks at Raf-Raf were sullen, those of the prisoners at Porto Farina were incandescent with resentment.

Cape Farina rouses pleasant shudders over the Barbary pirates. We are far removed from the days when walking the plank, the *bastinado* and the *hazzouk*, a lifetime manacled to the oars, ransom, rape, and forced concubinage were real possibilities of Mediterranean travel, or even of living near the coast. Only a century and a half ago, piracy was big business, the principal industry of Tunisia. The corsair crews were international, many of them renegades from Europe or Christian communities in the East. They paid a fixed percentage of the spoils to the local rulers for the use of ports and harbours and for the facilities of their markets for disposing of treasure and slaves. Some became freebooting admirals—*amir al-bahar*, or lord of the sea—in service of the expanding Ottoman empire. A few, like the Barbarossa brothers, seized political power and ruled in Algiers and Tunis under nominal Turkish sovereignty. The line between piracy and legitimate warfare was probably never so clearly drawn for contemporaries as it may seem to us. The early Moorish raids against the Spanish coast were made to free their co-religionists held there as slaves or to seize property that the expelled Arabs considered their own. Byzantines and Arabs preyed on each other's shipping and provinces as part of the struggle for empire. Barbary pirates were even enlisted in the internecine wars of Christendom. That most Christian King Francis I kept Kheireddine Barbarossa as his guest in Marseilles for a year to attack Spanish ships. Kheireddine, whose name meant "The Good of Religion", objected to the ringing of the Christian church bells of Marseilles, and got them silenced. He spent the years of his retirement building a great mosque, and he is still revered as a hero of Islam.

Piracy was not confined to one race or religion, nor to a single period. The Homeric Greeks accepted it as a means of livelihood in the Aegean. Julius Caesar was captured by Adriatic corsairs as a boy. The Vandals founded a kingdom on it. Norman, Aragonese, and Genoese "crusaders" attacked the coasts of Tunisia in what to an objective observer look very like pirate raids. It is questionable whether the inhabitants of La Goulette and Tunis saw a great difference in being sacked by the forces of Charles V or of the Turks. The Barbary pirates were merely the last, and most successful, in a long line of such appearances.

Do we connive with evil by finding such outbreaks exciting, even glamorous? We would certainly not want to return to them, but would we forego the excitement of the past if we could undo the cruelty, suffering, and degradation? Would we really like to see history an edifying succession of clean elections, reform bills, and people dying in bed? No; we are relieved of moral responsibility for the past and may judge it aesthetically rather than ethically. Someone else has paid for our shudders.

With such thoughts in mind we drove out of the brooding

prison of Porto Farina and into the gathering dusk. At one of the narrow bridges we were stopped by a *gendarme*.

"You cannot pass," he said. "The bridge is blown up."

"Who did it?"

"*Fellaghas.*" This is an Arab word for bandits which the French used to cover both banditry and the guerrilla activities of the Nationalists. "You will have to go round the back way, by way of Bizerta."

The dark was coming on, and the back way was not marked on our map. "Is it safe?" we asked.

The *gendarme* shrugged. "Who knows?" he answered.

V. CAP BON AND THE NORTH

CAP BON REACHES TOWARD EUROPE LIKE AN OUT-STRETCHED hand. The Italian island of Pantelleria is due east, less then fifty miles away, and Sicily can be sighted on a clear day. Geologically it is in fact a part of Europe—a continuation of the Sicilian range, and not of the Atlas that begins across the bay. Cap Bon has a real Land's End quality of rolling fields gradually subsiding into wild stretches of heather and broom that peter out in rocky shores and pockets of sand. The Arabs live chiefly on the coast: in Korbous, a thermal station and pleasure resort on the bay, with the unreal look of a resort town and people soft and flattering like bath-house attendants; or in Kelibia on the sea, a more convincing place founded by Sicilian Greeks three hundred years before Christ and frequently sacked throughout history, whose inhabitants are fishermen, salty and weather-beaten from the different kinds of exposure. But the heart of the cape is farmland planted with cereals and vines and red-roofed farm houses. Driving across it, you would think you were in some gently heaving, wide-skyed part of Europe.

Roxane took me to a picnic on Cap Bon, a gathering of *colons*, the French farmers and land-owners of North Africa. The picnic was held on the vast, partly wild estate of a Frenchman on Cap Bon; it was an annual event and the *colons* attended *en masse* from their farms and properties all over northern Tunisia, converging in jeeps, station wagons, Citroëns, a few from nearby farms on horse-back. The men dressed in riding breeches or corduroy trousers and loose jackets with leather patches to cushion a gun; their faces were tanned below and white above, the colour of men who work, rather than play, out of doors. The women wore tweeds good enough to last a lifetime, and their faces were chary of make up. There were lots of children and dogs, and a grateful number of *jeunes filles en fleur*. Older boys and young men were rare—away at school, or in the Army. Tunisian *colons* maintained close ties with France, educating their children there and going home every year they could afford it. They spoke the French of France and looked down a little on their Algerianised compatriots to the west. A lot of the paraphernalia of *la belle France*—a sprinkling of titles, le Yacht Club, *chinoiserie* and Balmain gowns, irregular *ménages* and *maris complaisants*, the Galeries Lafayette, le Bal des Petits Lits Blancs, mayoral weddings at the Hôtel de Ville, the Army, the Church, and the deeply divisive politics— had been transplanted whole to Barbary.

Roxane knew the names, not of every individual, but of all the families and clans at the picnic. Many were related, or bewilderingly connected by marriage, divorce, and re-arrangement of spouses. The picnic broke into natural groups of families, friends, and generations. There were exchanges of the abundant country-style food everyone had brought. After lunch we watched some falcons which the host brought out and set to hunting small birds. Some of the men went shooting. Not an Arab, not even a chauffeur or a game keeper, was in sight.

Roxane introduced me to two *colon* families who became friends of mine. One was a handsome young couple named de P—— who had a neighbouring farm on Cap Bon; the other a large comfortable clan named Du—— with married and unmarried children and their ramifications, who farmed a large domaine in the Mejerda Valley in the north west.

Roger de P—— had inherited his farm from his grandfather

who was a famous general and had been granted the land during the first days of the French occupation. At the time most of the fertile land belonged to members of the Bey's court, who were glad to sell out for cash to pay their debts and keep up their establishments in Tunis or La Marsa. Not all French-owned land was acquired so scrupulously. Protectorate policy aimed to turn Tunisia into a strong, free commune of French land-owners: large tracts, often inefficiently farmed by the Arabs or used only for tribal grazing, were alienated and given to the *colons*, a device which also created a useful labour pool of the dispossessed natives. It was an age of efficiency and progress and Darwinian economics; the same sort of thing was being done to the Indians of America. But the present holders of the land were of the second and third generation, and their roots were deep in what they considered their own soil.

You could always tell a Frenchman's farm, even from the road. There was a certain formality, the visible sign of taste, that great invention of the French which operates in everything they do. An Arab or Italian farm might be more flourishing, even more beautiful, but it never looked like the conscious symbol of a whole civilisation. The de P——'s farm had the earthy elegance of a setting for Molière. An avenue of dusty pink tamarisks led from the gate. The house, tall and man-sarded, appeared to rest lightly on the ground as if it had just landed and was undecided whether to stay or go. A rose garden, formal and graceful as a minuet, marched round two sides of the house; and in the distance a line of eucalyptus pretended to be poplars. Roger de P—— rode about his *hectares* daily, supervising the planting and harvests, checking pumps, testing the wine, discussing work schedules with his Arab foreman, and making plans for the future. His wife had a careless, almost prodigal beauty. She had had a brief career on the stage, but had settled down, with an enthusiasm that matched her husband's, to the life of a farmer's wife. She raised three children,

Korbous

looked after the house and flower garden, drilled a Tunisian cook in *haute cuisine*, dressed like a Parisienne, and entertained perfectly. The structure of their lives was at the mercy of drought, locusts, the market, and the vagaries of politics. This precariousness sharpened their enthusiasm like salt in food.

The Du——s were a much older couple who had come to Tunisia themselves after the best land had been colonised. But hard work and frugal living created the domain that supported them, their children and grandchildren and would, they hoped, support the children of their grandchildren.

The Mejerda is the one full-time river in Tunisia; though wildly seasonal in flow, it never dries up completely as the *wedds* do in the summer drought. The country is fortunate but by no means lush. The landscape concentrates on essentials: the hills bald, the riverbanks untrimmed, the fields quietly prosperous, like rich Quakers. Huge, co-operative silos, visible for miles, complete and concentrate the air of comfort and security, as castles complete a landscape of strife. The roads are excellent and almost undisturbed by traffic; long valleys and undifferentiated hills stretch westward with a feeling of endless, continental space. In this rather Texas-like landscape, the Du——s' farm was also unmistakably French, but in a different style from the de P——s'. The entrance lay between the stables and a private chapel. Not that the Du——s were particularly horsey or religious; these things were a matter of course and in their early days here they had had to provide for themselves. The house was low and unassuming. The entrance lay through the kitchen; there were other doors, but they were blocked off by furniture or disuse. The kitchen was the most important room anyway; the other rooms had an air of having been added later according to need. Each room had a bed in it, for the family was large and elastic, and a huge Breton *armoire*. The nursery was a great bare barracks filled with cots and usually housing a flock of visiting grandchildren. The rest were always present in the mounted photographs that were the only decoration throughout the house.

M. Du——'s hair was white and his face two-toned. He smoked a pipe most of the time and watched life with the amused detachment of the slightly deaf. His amusement sometimes kindled to alarm when he realised what his wife might be committing him to. Mme. Du—— talked for both of them, in rapid French with enthusiastic fliers into English, which she had learned as a girl on long bus trips around the British Isles. Once, when giving Roxane a recipe for a grated cheese dish, she began: "First you rape your cheese." She wore her grey-blonde hair in a thick knot behind her head, and I used to think that whereas Roxane was Corinthian, Mme Du—— was built on the Doric order.

Mme. Du——'s principal interest, apart from her family, was food. When you went to their farm, you were expected to stay for at least two meals and to take away enough for several more. The kitchen was always fragrant with cauldrons of *ragôut* or *pot-au-feu*, mounds left to rise or rest, marinades, brews, and provisions of raw material. The larder was crammed as if for a seige. There was no trouble Mme. Du—— would not go to for a dish. Once I saw a rabbit hanging from a hook in the kitchen, blood slowly dripping from its eye into a pan below; it twitched and I realised, my stomach turning over, that it was being bled to death for some culinary necessity. Mme. Du—— ate little herself; food to her was a sacrament of communion with those she loved. If you did not come often to the farm, she came to you, laden like Ceres with baskets of home-made *pâté*, goat's milk cheese, fruit, vegetables, and flowers from the farm. When she visited friends she would go to the kitchen and turn out a batch of *quenelles* or meringues, or something else that would keep "for a case of urgency." It was as if she had been hungry during those early days and was determined that no one she knew would ever be so again.

Surfeited with food, we welcomed the customary walk round the farm, guided by M. Du—— and an unmarried son. First the pig-sties, scrubbed and disinfected daily, but stinking with the sweet ineradicable smell of swine. M. Du—— gazed with affection at the bloated skins and brutal folds, though they almost persuaded me to the Moslem horror of pork. From there, we crossed an irrigation ditch to a plain tufted like candlewick with grape vines cut to essential clumps, the tight bunches almost on the ground. The *vendange*, explained the young Du——, was pressed at a co-operative nearby, then shipped to France where, as "Algerian", it is mixed with French wines. For a long time under the Protectorate, grape culture had been restricted by law to protect French growers; when that hindrance had been removed, an epidemic of phylloxera had wiped out the vines, and they had had to be replaced by hardier American roots. As we walked farther on, the tufted spread became a striped blanket of different grains, stretching out as far as the eye could follow—not all their land, the Du——s explained; a son-in-law's property met theirs, and there were other, unrelated *colons* in the valley. We passed several Arab labourers who greeted us in a friendly, dignified fashion and engaged the young Du—— in fluent Arabic conversation about the work. They lived in a hamlet of clay *ghourbis* on the edge of a dry gully between two fields, where the women waved to us and the naked babies stared curiously. Circling back to the house, we recrossed the ditch into a grove of recently planted olives which would only begin to bear after young Du—— inherited the farm, and were therefore known as his trees. Then through a cosy slum of chicken huts, kitchen garden, flowers, and fruit trees, to find Mme. Du—— waiting at the kitchen door. "And now, after making that exercise, you will want high tea!"

Neither the Du——s nor the de P——s had any intimate Moslem friends, but this stemmed I think not from personal antipathy but from a profound difference in temper between the French and the Arabs. Mme. Du—— once said to me, "The Arabs are never vulgar; I wish I could say the same about my own countrymen." During the general strikes of 1952 and 1953, when the Tunisians had been ordered by their leaders to supply nothing to the *colons*, the tenants and labourers of both families saw that they got sugar, coffee, cigarettes, and anything else they did not produce themselves. Neither farm nor family was molested by *fellaghas*.

Some Frenchmen had not taken the trouble to earn Arab friendship and suffered for it. One case I knew stemmed from the sort of peasant meanness that provokes murder in Normandy and Provence, but without the racial or political aggravation. An Arab tenant worked a small triangle of land at the corner of a *colon's* property, cultivating every inch except the space occupied by the clay hut where he lived with his wife. The *colon* wanted to widen the road, a reasonable project from his view point, but one that would take a strip perhaps one foot wide from his tenant's bean patch. The Arab refused to allow it and kept watch day and night to prevent the work. The Frenchman thereupon went to court—a French court, as the law provided in cases involving the two nationalities. One Sunday morning as the *colon* came out of the village church with his young son in his arms, the Arab, no doubt desperate with fear for his land, darted up and stabbed the Frenchman in the back. The killer ran out of town toward the farm, some thought to finish the job by killing the *colon's* wife. He had several miles to run and almost made it, but was just overtaken by a police jeep. The *colon's* spinal column was severed and he died in a week. In the end the French court found in favour of the tenant, but by that time the Frenchman was dead, the Arab in prison for life, and another murder added to the dreary statistics of inter-racial strife.

Many of my friends were in danger during the insurrection.

Some were in a café in Sousse, assisting at the election of a Miss Tunisia, when the place was sprayed with machine-gun bullets, leaving two dead and several wounded. Life had that curiously illogical quality: one went to cafés, cinemas, parties, while bombs went off in the next street. Foreigners were not a target for either side. But many innocent victims were attacked as 'targets of opportunity' or just as a symbol of the enemy. One such mindless act of violence was directed against a French doctor I knew in a southern town. He was hard working, altruistic, and extremely fond of Tunisia and Tunisians; besides his ordinary practice among all nationalities, he ran a free clinic for the poor—which meant exclusively Moslems. Ironically he belonged to a liberal Catholic group which sympathised with Arab nationalism. One evening he was walking in his garden after work when a bullet blasted across the wall and into his pelvis. A ragged Arab was seen running across the fields but was never caught. The doctor lived to forgive his attacker and continue his devotion to Tunisia.

There were also counter-terrorists. Early one morning in December a man was driving to work from his home in a suburb of Tunis. A motor-car approached coming from the city. As they passed, the man's car was sprayed with bullets. Though wounded, he managed to stop the car and hide behind it in a ditch along the road. In a few minutes another car drove past, going toward Tunis. The wounded man hailed it. He appeared to know the people inside and climbed into the car with them. A few hours later his body was found, riddled with lead fired point blank, lying in a field the other side of Tunis.

The murdered man was Farhat Hached, a labour leader and leader of the Nationalists. There were witnesses to the attack— a shepherd who had been in a field near the road, and a passing truck driver. They were able to give details about the assassins' cars. Names were mentioned in the souks: a group of policemen, the son of a prominent lawyer, several *colons*. Other names were bruited at the Residency: the Communists, a son of the Bey, rival Nationalists. An article appeared in the French-controlled press stating that the crime was incompatible with the French character (this was about the time of the Dominici-Drummond affair). The police did nothing.

But the people did. The iron shutters clanged down over the shop fronts, ports and factories lay idle, transportation stopped, and the schools emptied of Tunisian children. The whole country closed down in a strike of mourning. Even the weather turned sullen: a grey migraine settled over the rooftops and cold rain descended on the silent, shuttered streets. French soldiers patrolled the city, and a few Arabs with *burnouses* over their heads huddled under the dripping eaves and looked at them with cold determined eyes.

North-western Tunisia was also a favoured field of Roman colonisation, and for the same reason. The *tell*, as these high plains and valleys are called, is littered with the débris of classical civilisation. Its bones lie whitening on the hillsides or half-buried in the fold of a valley. The plough continually turns up marble heads and limbs, and in some places the ground is so thick with coins it seems as if some crazy Midas had planted them expecting a monetary harvest. I liked best the isolated, unexpected bits not in the guide-books: a stone mill-wheel uncovered by recent rains in the bank of a *wedd*, a broken masonry arch screened in brambles and encrusted with snails, or some ambiguous block of stone with the marks of the chisel weathering back to a state of nature. Shards and fragments of the past that suit our modern need for the allusive and incomplete.

There are more impressive monuments to the Roman rationale that made Africa the bread-basket of Rome, uprooting the old diversified crops of olives, fruit, and cattle for the ever-expanding cultivation of grain. One of these is the aqueduct that carried water from springs in the flank of Mount Zagouan to the cisterns of Carthage. It dominates parts of the *tell* like a Piranesi nightmare. The ruined columns of rose-brown arches stride across the plains, step over river beds, and vanish into ridges and hills to emerge in the next valley or downward slope, still inflexibly on the march. The piers lengthen or shorten as the ground rises and falls beneath them, keeping the conduit at a steady decline so that the water would flow by gravity. Massive architecture is always oppressive, especially when confirmed by the ravages of time. The aqueduct is obsessive: it reappears again and again as you drive across the plains, and seems imbued with intelligence and will and a blind Roman determination to reach its goal. Even in ruin, with conduit broken and dry, the arches march implacably on, like those soldiers we are supposed to admire who stand obstinately at their posts in the face of disaster, or persist in the attack with their bowels half shot away.

Roman thoroughness can also be descried in the number of complete towns they built on the *tell*, where all the trappings of urban living—the forums, theatres, baths, temples, and fine houses—were reiterated where today there is only a farm, a *marabout's* tomb, or at most a comfortless village. Some of their names are preserved in a sort of linguistic amber: Tinja is ancient Thimida, Béjà was Vaga, and the mud *ghourbis* of Jebba contain the marble bones of Thigibba Bure. A few of their sites are still deeply imbued with the spirit of place. Utica, older than Carthage and once a seaport, has been drowned by the Mejerda River and now lies ten miles inland under fields of silt. Thuburba Maijus once obliterated nature itself with plains of mosaic, swollen temples, and over-triumphant arches; but history shrugged and tumbled Thuburba like a pack of cards. Bulla Regia has been buried under a leisurely landslide of grain upon grain over the centuries, and now seems secretive and slightly dotty, with roots growing out of the ceilings and nibbling sheep peering down at you

from the tops of arches and walls. And Dougga—well, time
has been kind to Dougga, and she deserves it. For Dougga is
the most beautiful of Roman African cities.

Thugga, to give her her ancient name, is built on a mountain
top and falls in terraces that look across a broad sweep of valley
to the High Tell beyond. The highest level was an acropolis
where the important buildings are disposed with an almost
Greek feeling for site. From the seats of the theatre, you see the
valley and the distant hills framed by the columns and archi-
trave of the stage, challenging backdrop to actor or play. The
years, instead of engulfing Thugga, have left it cleaner, sharper,
more exposed. A grove of olives, looking themselves more
stone than vegetable, flows through the town like a slow river,
bathing the feet of the monuments, flooding the foundations
with pools of light and shade. A homely touch is the public
latrine, still intact, with stone seats disposed in a sociable semicircle.

Thugga was in fact older than Roman colonisation and may
have antedated the Phoenicians. In the 2nd century B.C. it
was captured by the Numidian king Massinissa, who married
poor Sophonisba, a niece of Hannibal's, after defeating and
killing her previous husband, King Syphax. As a wedding
present Sophonisba received from Massinissa a cup of poison,
to spare her the shame of appearing at Rome in the triumph of
Scipio. A Punic-Libyan monument stands among the olive
trees of Thugga, symbolising the union of native and foreigner.

Dougga is still inhabited, or reinhabited. A sizeable village of
Berbers (read: Numidians) shelters among the ruins. They
have a decent little mosque and a *marabout* constructed of
Roman stones. The villagers look fairly prosperous and behave
politely to visitors, like hosts. Looking down from one tier of
Roman dwellings into the courtyard of another, we saw some
young men having a party. They were playing a flute and drum
and, I fear, drinking wine. We spoke to them and learned that

they were celebrating the wedding of one of them, which was taking place elsewhere. We said *mabrouk*, which is a blessing, and the groom, egged on by the others, did a dance in which he showed what he was going to do when he finally met his bride.

Near the northernmost point of Africa lies an inland lake connected by a channel to the sea. It makes one of the finest harbours in the world at a place where the world wants a harbour, and on this keel Bizerta has sailed triumphantly across the centuries, from Punic times to NATO. When I first saw it, Bizerta was also a ruin, the famous port clogged with sunken hulls and tangles of rusting iron, the streets and squares a wasteland of torn-up pavements and the metal viscera and crumbling yellow walls of houses, the work of British and American bombardments of 1942–43. But Bizerta has continually consumed its past in a series of urgent, practical presents. Not a single stone remains of Punic or Roman Hippo Diarrythus (the anatomical name apparently deriving from the channel that cuts the site in two). As Benzert it was a pirate port, later improved and fortified by the Dey of Algiers. The French and the Venetians each bombarded it in the 18th century. Since 1891 the French have developed it into a vast naval complex of moles and dry-docks, a pyrotechnic station, airfields, an arsenal at Ferryville, a web of strategic roads and recently a subterranean base tunnelled beneath the surrounding hills.

The ruins I first saw were quickly cleared away, the harbour unclogged, and along the battered streets a new town—with the lamentable name of Bijouville—sprang up, as French in looks and feel as Toulon or Marseilles. Ships of the Allied nations called there with old-fashioned fanfare and protocol, and receptions were held on board where snowy ensigns served champagne if the flag was French, Scotch and sherry if it was British, and fruit juice and coke if American. The ratings spent their time in the bars and backstreets of town, where Dirty Gerty and her sisters converted hard or soft currencies into sailors' souvenirs and solace.

Near Bizerta there still exists the remnant of a small private empire founded more than a century ago by an adventurous member of an Anglo-Irish family of ancient lineage. The younger branch established itself there in a Moorish palace set in a sort of rectory garden and surrounded by a park of olive, cypress, and pine. The men would sometimes dress in Arab clothes and sit in the *koubba*, or domed gazebo, receiving the neighbouring shaikhs or their tenants and villagers. Some of them served as British consuls for the port of Bizerta. The property, which was called Ben Negro, stretched from the coast through a good part of the hills surrounding the Lake of Bizerta. Little by little it had been nibbled away for the naval installations or for the municipality.

When I first saw it, Ben Negro was inhabited by the last of the family, a frail and charming maiden lady who lived there alone except for a one-eyed old servant who had been there since he was a boy. During the War, the palace and park had been occupied by the whole series of invaders: the Italians had taken all the furnishings; the Germans stripped the walls of panelling, including some that had been in Byron's study in Pisa; and the Americans had chopped down most of the olives and pines for firewood. When the troops had left, the owner came back and was able to gather enough furniture for two or three of the rooms. We used to visit her on Sunday afternoons and walk about the empty palace and damaged park, hearing about the spacious old days when the tennis court rang with the laughter of Irish and English cousins, or her father sat in the *koubba* exchanging silences with bedouin chiefs, or of the time when her grandparents had tea with the Bey of Tunis and were served a cake politely inscribed in sugar letters "Hurrah for Jesus Christ."

Close to the Algerian border is the tiny port of Tabarka, a depot and outlet for the cork that is stripped from oak trees in the forests that cover the foothills of the Atlas which rise west of Bizerta. The harbour is closed off by a volcano-shaped island; and on its summit is the ruin of a castle that recalls yet another private dream of empire. In 1504 the Genoese family of Lomellini obtained a concession to collect coral along this coast. They made the island their depot, built the castle, garrisoned it with a private army, and remained there for the next two centuries. One wonders what relationship existed between the Renaissance Italians on the island and the Barbary Moslems on shore. Was there trade, a wary friendship, even social intercourse; or a strict embargo broken by violent incidents? You can easily swim the distance between, and it is hard to believe that in two hundred years some disgruntled Genoese soldier did not desert and go to join the pirates, or an escaped slave seek refuge and possible repatriation on the island. We hired a fishing boat with its piratical-looking owner to take us round the island and along the coast a short way to see the needles of rock carved by the waves. The castle itself was a military area and could not be visited; but we disembarked on a little beach and found a meaningless scrabble of ruins, perhaps a Genoese boat-shed or storehouse for coral, at the foot of the hill. The water was clear as air along the shore, and the boatman scraped sea urchins off the bottom, cracked them like nuts, and offered us the salty pulp.

Farther off the coast, out of sight and also out of bounds, lay the islands of La Galite. A few hardy fishermen live on them and catch excellent lobster for the markets of Tunis. La Galite was best known, however, as the place where the French Government imprisoned a Nationalist politician named Habib Bourguiba.

VI. HAMMAMET

IT WAS CHRISTMAS, AND I WAS INVITED TO SPEND THE HOLIDAY at Hammamet.

Hammamet is a name of many associations in Tunisia, of beauty, luxury, pleasure, and—for those who disapprove of those things—wickedness. It is, first of all, a fishing village on the east coast about an hour's drive from Tunis, facing on a wide sandy beach and surrounded by orchards of lemons, oranges, and pomegranates. It is also a colony of international expatriates, individuals who had in common taste, leisure, and a love of beauty, and who had separately discovered this harbour in the ' twenties and had come to live here. They had built simple, lovely houses in fabulous gardens, and retired behind the tabias—walls of earth planted with prickly pear and aloes—to lead lives of quiet felicity. An invitation to Hammamet was therefore irresistible.

My hosts were an Anglo-American couple. Vee was a witty, cultivated Englishwoman who spoke and dressed with chic understatement. Her husband, Jay, liked to describe himself as a hillbilly; his taste was exuberant and he spoke in hyperbole. When they had first come to Hammamet twenty-five years before, there had been nothing on their land but wild fields and the deserted beach. Together they had created a house, a garden, and a way of life in which Georgian simplicity and Baroque extravagance were mingled in a highly personal style.

There are people who charge everything they touch with excitement: nothing to them is neutral, everything loved or hated, prized or rejected, for or against, enchanting or monstrous. Vee and Jay had this power. They placed a high value on every ingredient of their lives, and because of this, everything became uniquely valuable. I had visited their house once or twice before. The shell was as simple and satisfactory as an egg's: two hollow squares set side by side with an open court in the centre of each. The walls were bare and undecorated, the ceilings vaulted, the whole whitewashed inside and out. Against this plain and lovely background, English walnut furniture, Venetian gilt mirrors, marble tables, a T'ang horse, Victorian knicknacks, lamps and vases by Giacometti, African shields and masks, and everywhere fragments of Greece and Rome lived together in perfect harmony. The white walls and high ceilings allowed every object its own value and modulated their contrasts and discrepancies into a quiet discourse, spiked with occasional epigrams, on the vagaries of taste. Dominating everything in profusion were flowers and leaves, grown in the garden and brought lovingly indoors to be displayed like precious jewels, in blazing fountains of spray, cornucopias of colour, basins of heady or subtle scent, or sometimes just a rare and perfect bloom. A pack of Burmese cats, sable-coated and emerald eyed, stalked this Fabergé jungle, and in one of the patios a red and green parrot lorded it over a cote of white doves. More important than the rarity, value, or beauty of each object, or even the taste that brought them together, was the unmistakable patina of things that are loved.

Even people came in for this appreciation. Vee and Jay's friends seemed to shine with heightened lustre, polished by their attention and affection. Everyone felt a little more brilliant, witty, or attractive in their presence and esteem. This may account for my somewhat dazzled recollection of the Christmas party. The other guests were a French film actress, the local *caïd* and his wife, another Arab who had a farm in the south, a Paris *couturier*, a nobleman from Florence, an English girl who was spending the winter in Tunisia, Roxane of course, and some of the neighbours from Hammamet.

The French actress, I remember, was all topaze tones, from the crown of her chestnut hair to the tips of her lemon slippers. She had reached the age when Frenchwomen are most attractive and when age no longer matters. When she laughed (no Frenchwoman ever smiles) her amber eyes cast a net of tiny beige wrinkles down her cheeks and her apricot lips stretched in a closed, feline V. She seemed to recognise an affinity with the Burmese cats who mingled with the guests, and caressed them with coral fingertips.

The *caïd* wore a silken robe embroidered with gold; his wise, weary eyes were set in a young, not very intelligent face. His wife was dark and smouldering and dressed in black. The Arab farmer was one of the handsomest men I had ever seen; he wore tweed and had an air of having strayed from his natural habitat, and he escaped early before the party was over. The *marchese* was worldly and at the same time completely insulated from the world.

Among the neighbours of the expatriate colony was an ancient pre-Raphaelite beauty with long red hair and violet-shadowed eyes whose conversation was redolent with memories of Yeats and Shaw. Another was an American painter who had been on the staff of a snob magazine in Paris during the twenties. He had never lost his wide-eyed Middle Western wonder at the scenes of high life he had been admitted to, and because of this his reminiscences of the first Diaghilev ballet or a black-and-white ball at the Comtesse de C's were as funny and unpretentious as his story about the incontinent coloured girl he went to school with in Iowa.

The white drawing room was swooning with flowers that evening. The Burmese cats prowled round our feet with mesmeric emerald eyes or stretched like sphynxes on a convenient ledge. For dinner we ate roast peacock, which lent a Lucullan

House at Hammamet

note, and afterwards danced to spirited waltzes and faded fox-trots played by Roxane at the piano. Toward the end of the evening I danced with the English girl and found her the nicest person in the room. When the neighbours left we had a last glass of champagne before going to bed.

I was put to sleep on a couch in the library, a small octagonal room lined with bookshelves and capped with a white dome, like a *marabout's* tomb. I scanned the shelves as I undressed. There were sets of Austin, Trollope, Proust, and James, and big portfolios on flowers and gardens, their leather bindings and gilt lettering worn by generations of palms. But what interested me most was a collection of the incunabula of the 1920's, editions of the Nonesuch and Shakespeare Press, Virginia Woolf and Gertrude Stein, Ronald Firbank, early Hemingway, the Paris edition of *Ulysses,* the *Tropics*, and a cupboard full of *Verves* and *Minotaurs*. I lay reading till dawn, interred like a *marabout* in the dust of a still fragrant past.

The gardens of Hammamet are known on both sides of the Mediterranean, and Vee and Jay's was one of the finest. French visitors used to exclaim, "*C'est le paradis terrestre!*" and searchers for an English phrase usually came up with "a garden of Eden." It was the only image that sufficed. After the sunstruck landscape and metallic road from Tunis, the green shadows, the scent of lemon blossoms, jasmine, and broom, the blessed sight and sound of water—all struck with the poignancy of something refound.

First of all, it is a working garden : there are chickens among the peacocks and beehives near the roses. Strawberries, salads, and Jerusalem artichokes come out of the kitchen garden. At harvest time, families of bedouin perch in the branches picking fruit, and crates of yellow-green lemons or purple-green olives block the paths. Against this utilitarian background, nature has been encouraged to compose her rarest poetry. Cypress trees stand stiff as black-suited grandees wreathed in jasmine or trumpet flowers. A grove of bamboo trails green feather across a path. Hibiscus blow red trumpets in the shade, and poinsettias brandish handfuls of red or pink stars. Lotus and water lilies rise, pink as sunrise over the Ganges, blue as twilight on the Nile, from still pools. The air at day is scented with verbena, pinks, sweet geraniums, and mint; at night the creamy horns of datura, limp in the sunlight, rise and impregnate the dark with rapturous perfume. The garden blossoms in metal and stone: a twisted black column veiled in clematis, a marble sarcophagus holding a resurrection of bulbs, freesias drooping from a pair of bronze urns, and some battered heads and limbs that do nothing, but simply are, like the flowers and leaves.

The sight and sound of water is part of the refreshment of the garden. A windmill straddles the deep, pure well, and water runs through canals, splashes in basins, leaps in fountains, or lies in mirror-like pools. None is wasted, all is on its way to some seed or root, or to nourish the passing bedouin and their cattle that stop to drink at the trough outside the gate.

Two Arab gardeners helped Vee and Jay to tend this paradise. One of them was old now, almost blind and reputedly syphilitic, but every morning he reported for work and dutifully kissed Jay on the cheek and Vee on the hands. They would never think of curbing this ritual, though Vee kept a bottle of disinfectant handy and slipped inside to wash in it afterwards. Jay could not be bothered: he loved dirt and water and everything natural. I have watched him pack the loam around a root tenderly and crumble a goat's pellet between his fingers and sniff to see if it was sweet. Once an officious visitor asked, "What is your profession?" Jay cast him a cold eye and answered, "The oldest."

When the War invaded this paradise, Vee and Jay refused to break and run, but tried to live on quietly in the confusion of the Vichy era. One day shortly after the Axis occupied

Tunisia, a pair of German soldiers armed with machine guns marched into the garden where Jay was working. "Darling," he said to Vee, "these bastards have come to arrest me; show no emotion." He went into the house and changed from blue jeans to a London suit, and was taken away—first to the Kasbah in Tunis, then to Naples, finally to a prison camp in Silesia. Vee was left alone with the old gardener. The Germans moved into the house, and Vee slept in a servant's room. At night her German guests got drunk and amused themselves by shooting at her door. Finally, she could stand no more and taking Coco, the red and green parrot, she moved to the village and stayed with Arab friends. When Hammamet was liberated by the British, she moved back into the house and waited for Jay. The war finally ended in Europe and the prisoners were released. Jay came back and found Vee and the old gardener where he had last seen them, on the path near the garden gate.

In the prison hospital where malnutrition and a lung infection landed him, Jay had kept himself going by remembering the past and planning for the future. In his mind he built the second square of the house and the white drawing room, laid out new beds of flowers, and planted more fruit trees. When he got back, he and Vee wiped out the negation of the War by enlarging, improving, and creating even more beauty than they had had before. Jay collected plants from gardeners all over the world. A new species sent him into a fever of desire, anticipation, and activity. One day I came upon him in the rose garden among hundreds of kinds and colours—yellow, coral, crimson, purple, cream, mauve—of that most satisfying and obliging of flowers. "Look!" he called in a voice hoarse with rapture, "a *grey* rose."

He held a flower in his earth-stained hand. It was a perfectly formed, half open rose, neither white nor cream nor tinged with the slightest blush, but a pure, pale grey—a rose *en grisaille*.

.   .   .   .   .

The beach at Hammamet is the kind of beach one always looks for but rarely finds—broad, sandy, tideless, deserted. It is a place for long lonely walks, for picking up rare shells and mysterious bits of flotsam, for swimming naked and bemused in a crystal ether of water, sand, and air, and for lying in the sun for hours with the mind swept clean of thoughts, desires, or even identity. A jelly fish floats by, and one feels as aimless and transparent as he. A bird soars overhead and one shares his weightlessness. In the distance a black speck appears. Is it a sea bird, a donkey, or a man?—or is this one of those unfocused moments when a bit of dust on one's own eyeball becomes a figure moving in the landscape or an object falling through the air? The speck moves but gets no larger. You shut your eyes or turn away. When you look again it has disappeared—perhaps it never existed, or was going away and is now out of sight. But from an invisible fold of sand or dent in the shore, it appears again. Now you can see it is human, but whether man, woman, or child is impossible to tell. It is wrapped in heavy robes, the Arab's protection against the sun. You lie back, still alone in the discreteness of space. Suddenly the figure is within a few hundred feet and you see it is a woman and cover yourself. She is carrying her shoes, soft leather *babouches*, in one hand, and a basket of eggs in the other. You look away and do not speak, and she passes without a glance—are you invisible? have you ceased to exist?—and plods steadily on toward the village. If it is a child or a man you cover up too, for the Arabs are modest, but you say, "*Essalam alaikum*"—peace be on you— and he replies, "*Wa alaikum essalam*"—and on you peace. He too is carrying his shoes, if he has any, and perhaps a net or a line, and his catch. He may stop and have a cigarette but he does not talk much for the Arabs are not embarrassed by silence. If it is a child and you ask him his name, he will reply, "Abdallah", which means slave of God and is a real name but probably not his. Then he will pick up his shoes and his fish (is there an angel beside him?) and walk on past you, retreating not gradually, but in little jumps, suddenly becoming a black speck again— a bird, a donkey, or a man?—and vanish all at once, like a light put out. Time—if only one had that time, a whole afternoon to take some eggs to market or bring home the morning's catch, a whole life to walk along this beach, to smoke a cigarette in silence, to float in this clear sea. You look at your watch: it is time to go in and dress for the trip back to town.

I used to stay at other houses in the colony, each embowered in its particular paradise, guarded by tabias sharp as the neighbours' tongues. All had been built by the village masons in the same chaste native style, but the whitewashed walls accepted everything no matter how foreign, idiosyncratic, or bizarre, and accorded each object and personality a polite hearing. The houses differed one from another as if they were the lairs of a different species of animal.

One has been called by people of experience and discernment one of the most beautiful houses of the 20th century. It is a horizontal, understated structure, from which all colour is excluded. The exterior and lower floor are white, the upper storey a black *mesharabiyyah*; inside all is white, black, and *tête-de-nègre*. The rooms are almost bare: the proportion of space, the disposition of arch, window, and door speak without interruption. A few precious objects—a crystal ball, a rug of snow leopard, a bronze cat from the pyramids—fill the space around them with the quiet eloquence of perfection. Even in the garden, black-hued trees predominate—cypress and *karoub*—and only white flowers are permitted to grow. All is stark, austere, abstract—the perfection not of an egg, but of a sphere.

The house of the American painter was one huge room, a sky-lit studio and a barn for storing hundreds of canvases stacked against the walls. He collected colours the way other people collect stamps or butterflies. Outside the door was a democratic riot of geraniums, zinnias, and nasturtiums; inside a welter of objects taken for their purely visual value, the skin of a *pomelo,* a length of cheap shimmery rayon, a leaf, a piece of local pottery, a feather, or a shell. We used to sit around in front of the gaping corner fireplace in wintertime wrapped in paint-stained *burnouses,* or in the courtyard in our bathing suits in summer, laughing over a gin and grapefruit juice at a tale of Iowa, Paris, or the gaudier days of Hammamet. From his varied experience, the painter had distilled a number of sound aphorisms: "Between thirty and sixty everyone is the same age." "Frenchwomen invented chic because their noses are too long." About the French. "They don't care what you do in the bedroom as long as you don't do it in the *salon.*" About American girls. "What a screw would do."

The cottage of the pre-Raphaelite beauty was furnished with Fabian contempt for comfort and a dwindling income. The rich past was represented by a few priceless books and drawings, the meagre present by painted wood furniture and thin bedouin rugs. One house was all Louis XV and *chinoiserie* like an apartment on the Ile-Saint Louis. Another iterated the clichés of determined originality—goat skins, drift wood, and percussive colours. Still another was crammed with family portraits by Sargent, and immersed in a dim Jamesian twilight and pools of polished mahogany and silver.

Some of the happiest moments of my life were spent in what I guess must be called wasting time—that greatest of all luxuries—combing the beach, ruminating in the garden, or musing in the circular library. Vee and Jay were perfect hosts, making no demands on their guests other than to be agreeable and on time for meals. Sometimes we made short excursions in the neighbourhood: to Nabeul, a town of potters, weavers, and iron-workers; or to another village whose name I have forgotten, but whose blue-washed houses with strings of brilliant red peppers festooned to dry are unforgettable; or to a ruin in the hills, a lonely triumphal arch at the mouth of a valley and a castle on the heights, which Jay called Aphrodisium and said was connected with Belisarius. In the evenings we met for drinks under a pepper tree on the terrace, or before the fire in the white drawing-room. I remember one evening before the fire when Vee was sewing or mending something, Jay was singing Negro spirituals at the piano in a sweet, cracked voice, and the English girl and I, each with a Burmese cat on our knees, were playing canasta. Vee suddenly looked up from her work and remarked. "This must be one of those orgies at Hammamet."

The other Hammamet, the Arab town, is partly scattered among the orchards in one-family farms or little hamlets, partly strung in fishermen's huts along the coast, and partly crammed inside a little yellow fortress on a rocky promontory that closes the gulf to the north. A network of dirt lanes runs between the different hamlets. Through them old men in turbans and women wrapped to the eyes in black woollen *ha'iks* ride side-saddle on the hind half of donkeys; the b'r'r'ring of a bicycle bell warns you of traffic round the high blind corners of prickly pear; and great two-wheeled carts loaded with fresh dung or crates of oranges creak past driven by coppery young men in sweat-faded *chechias* and baggy pants. One of these lanes leads to a Moslem graveyard overlooking the beach. The graves were heaps of stones laid at random, and the maritime scilla grew among them, in spring a green cabbage that withers and dies in the summer sun, and in the autumn reappears as a single tall stalk, powdery mauve with a hundred tiny white stars blossoming upward to the tip—surely a symbol of immortality as affecting as the ragged asphodel.

A third of the population lives packed inside the yellow

fortress; with the white houses rising above the walls it looked from down the beach like a toasted *vol-au-vent* with cream filling. The east coast of Tunisia is studded with these miniature castles which were meant to protect the townspeople from pirates and crusaders alike. The castles were often captured, however, and held for a time by Spaniards, Italians, or Turks; and the people of Hammamet show in a certain fineness of feature and style of living the advantages of international connections, no matter how painfully acquired. Even today the fishing fleet that beaches on the sand beneath the castle walls—the boats blue, red, and orange, the nets stained tobacco brown—has an international flavour of Sicily and Pantelleria.

Under the Protectorate there were two garrisons in the neighbourhood, so wildly different in origin that they made me think of Hannibal's collection of Numidians, Celts, and Ligurians, or the troops of Thracians, Goths, and Masagetic Huns that Belisarius led this way. Outside the town was a contingent of Senegalese, the regularity of whose black beauty and arrowy limbs made them seem a race of pure-bred animals, bringing a rank odour of the jungle into town. The Arabs did not like them: they had the reputation of obeying orders—any orders. And in the fortress of Hammamet itself was a detachment of what in many ways is the modern equivalent of the Barbary pirates. The Foreign Legion is perhaps the world's last clean slate, asking a man no questions about his origin or past, not even his real name, and accepting renegades, rejects, and adventurers from anywhere. After the War it was flooded with recruits from a new race of Vandals, blue-eyed, yellow haired men who came out of the desert and kasbahs of Africa when the fighting ceased. They were taken into the Foreign Legion without question and fought for France in Korea, Indo-China, and again in Africa, where they did the dirtiest jobs with great efficiency. Under their *képis*, they used to stride about Hammamet, bored and nervous, their pale eyes reflecting another sky, their accents rustling like the leaves of a northern forest. The Arabs avoided them all and lived their warm, communal life in the hamlets, fishing villages, and castle walls.

Is individualism a Western invention? The question was posed vividly by the expatriates of Hammamet. The Arabs seem never to have developed such a degree of personal independence. An Arab does not act for himself in most things, nor on his own responsibility. "I will ask my father," a grown man will say when pressed for a decision, or "I will discuss it with my family." An Arab is at his most characteristic, and therefore most effective, as a member of a group—a family, a clan, or nowadays a committee. Decisions are made by the group and the individual fits in where he is most useful. Thus an arranged marriage is not galling, for it is part of a whole system of such arrangements—the kind and degree of education he gets, his profession, where he makes his home. Arab wisdom, the everyday common sense that rules his life, is communal too: originality is not a virtue: there is a proverb for every contingency, a formula for every occasion, a taboo for every misstep. An Arab therefore speaks with tremendous authority, even when he is wrong, and acts with the certainty of experience, not his own, but of the generations. They are puzzled by our social fragmentation and apparent isolation. "Are all Americans orphans?" one asked me. They could not understand the position, the *category*, of American girls travelling alone in Tunisia; and voluntary expatriation is a mystery to them.

Perhaps we are getting more like them. The expatriate colony of Hammamet was founded in the 1920's, the last outburst of originality we have known. That *dernier cri* is a faint echo in the world at large, but in the soft air and behind the tabias of Hammamet its standards have been preserved, as Elizabethan speech patterns are said to survive in the Kentucky mountains, or medieval witchcraft in the Black Forest. Some of it seems quaint today. It is one's duty to *épater le bourgeois*. The Delphic imperative is not Know, but Be Thyself. The rest of the world never caught up with the *avant garde*: it turned a corner and left them way out front. It was an attractive, gallant vanguard, and we have chosen a duller path than where it led. Perhaps today only in Hammamet can one still cultivate a grey rose.

The English girl went home in the spring. After she had gone, I said to Roxane, "I think I'd like to marry her."

Roxane looked thoughtful. Then, always practical, she got out a pack of cards to see what they had to say about it. Roxane had acquired a small reputation as a sybil by predicting marriages, love affairs, and a divorce or two among her friends; as most of Roxane's friends came to her for sympathy and advice, the cards had probably had help from her intuition. She had read my cards before, turning up such items as a letter from across water, a voyage, or a surprise in three days, three weeks, or three somethings. Not surprisingly, they usually came true. But this was more serious. She laid out the cards with an air of intense concentration. Soon a look of annoyance crossed her face.

"Damn," she muttered. "Cut again."

I did, and Roxane laid out the mystic pattern slowly. Try as she might, the queen of hearts came nowhere near the jack of clubs. A black queen kept coming in between.

"I think I'll ask her anyway," I said.

Jamila, I might explain here, had gone her own way some time before. Her disappearances had become longer and more frequent, and though she mentioned visits to her family, I had seen her once in La Marsa with a young Bey. We parted by mutual consent, but not without the drama that befitted the proprieties in such affairs.

I went to England, proposed, and was accepted. The wedding

had to be delayed for various reasons, and I returned to Tunisia alone. Laila was ebullient and gave me arcane advice on how to insure conception the first night and frequently thereafter. I began looking for a larger house in Sidi-bou-Saïd and at last found one halfway down the cliff, with rather primitive plumbing, no roof on the kitchen, but a superb view. It was Christmas again by the time we were married.

We returned from the honeymoon and spent a weekend at Hammamet. We were given a room that had its own door to the garden. Violets and narcissi were in bloom, and freesias pushed up through the cracks in the terrace outside the door. The morning sun streamed through the open windows, and through the door we could see the lemon trees and roses and hear the sound of waves on the sandy shore. It was as near as we will get to *le paradis terrestre*.

VII. THE *SAHEL*

SOUTH FROM HAMMAMET THE COASTLINE CURVES IN A LONG
shallow S that is known simply as the *Sahel*, or shore: a narrow
coastal strip, no more than twelve miles wide, of olive orchards and small mixed farms, market towns and fishing ports,
and cities neither swollen nor decayed but of proper size and
activity to balance the countryside. The *Sahel* reminded me of
that oriental story of the farmer who died and left a will saying
that a treasure was buried under his land; whereupon his sons
so dug and sifted the soil, that the land responded and produced a fortune in harvests. The prosperity of the *Sahel* is the
result of luck and labour.

The luck is fertile soil, heavy dews, and the sea, but centuries of thought and labour have gone to develop it. Crooked
ranks of olive trees hobble down the hillsides to the sea. Some
slopes are purposely left bare to collect and channel the sparse
rains. The overflow collects in *sebkhas*, or shallow lagoons,
where evaporation produces salt that is shovelled into snowy
hillocks to be used or sold. The fishing fleets harrow the
coastal waters for tunny, sardines, octopus, and sponge. Oil
presses and fish canneries process this harvest on the spot. In
the towns, traditional industries of silk and woollen weaving,
gold embroidery, basketry, and metal work are carried on.

This close-meshed economy was hardly penetrated by
colonialism; and there are few large estates or absentee land-
lords. Such self-sufficiency has bred a special character, shrewd,
industrious, and independent. Through the centuries, the

125

Sahel has shrugged off the authority of the north, whether Arab, Turkish, or French. Most of the leaders of Tunisian independence come from the *Sahel*.

Sousse, the capital of the region, is nicknamed "the smiling city." The old town sits jauntily on a hill overlooking the sea, caparisoned in crenellated walls and battlements which, though clearly built against some threat of violence, look gay and playful, as medieval dress looked too, even when it was defensive. Modern Sousse basks on the shore below, relaxed and genial, but not sunk in reveries of a famous past. The port is alive with the bustle of commerce, fishing boats, and pleasure craft; and the businessmen of Sousse—Arabs, Italians, Maltese, Jews—like to conduct their affairs standing under the shade trees on the esplanade or sipping a coffee or *gazeuse* in a café. Along the main street groups of square-shouldered youths munch fried watermelon seeds and jostle the dark-eyed girls coming from the cinema. Up in the old city, the alleys flap with the colourful laundry of the poor. The souks blossom with artificial flowers and sleazy silks in ravishing, unstable colours, and rows of blue and red painted pots. One artistic butcher used to decorate the hind quarters of every sheep with a *boutonnière* in a logical if unexpected spot. Throughout the city, radios at full blare create the ambiance necessary for Mediterranean contentment. In the *quartier reservé* the licentious soldiery used to bargain loudly with kimono-clad girls standing in the doorways of their one-room cribs.

I believe that the sunny disposition of Sousse descends from ancient times. The Punic city was at least as old as Carthage but it escaped the destruction of the Romans. Under the Emperor Trajan, the town was raised to the rank of colony with the resounding name of Colonia Ulpia Trajana Augusta Frugifera Hadrumetum. There are pleasant memories of "fruitful Hadrumetum" in a little museum under the kasbah. Among the

statues are a young Negro, a sleeping Cupid, and a mannekin-
pis. A stucco bas-relief shows a young man hesitating between
military *virtus* and a muse. Among the vivid mosaics are a
head of Medusa and a judgement of Neptune and Minerva.
Most of the mosaics emphasise the pleasures of the world:
fruit and flowers, fish from the sea, wild animal hunts, a bull
fighting a bear, portraits of a favourite racehorse and a cham-
pion gladiator, actors in masks. Some of the delights of the
flesh are translated into legend: there is depicted a triumph of
Bacchus, the rape of Ganymede, and the romping of satyrs and
nymphs. The unfaded colours and forthright design of the
mosaics give a startling immediacy to this extrovert pagan
world. The fish are recognisably the same species still caught
here; the rosy bronze flesh is the complexion of Sahelians today; the smiling cruelty to animals seems ineradicable; and
the nymphs and satyrs still romp in the *quartier reservé*.

Vandals, Byzantines, and Arabs came, knocked down and
rebuilt the walls, and changed the city's name to Huneri-
copolis, Justianopolis, and finally Sus. The Arabs embarked
from here for the conquest of Malta, Sicily, and southern
Italy; it was the port for their inland capital of Kairwan. The
ribat is one of the most important monuments of the Moslem
world. Half fortress and half monastery, the institution of the
ribat suited the militant piety of early Islam. *Ribats* were erected
up and down this coast for defence against the Byzantine fleet,
as they were on other frontiers, such as Spain or Palestine,
where Islam had to defend or extend itself by force. The garrisons were composed of men called *murabits*, who took vows
to defend the faith and, in addition to their military duties,
engaged in prayer and study to prepare for martyrdom. As
peace and mysticism changed the character of Islam, the religious life of the *ribats* became more important than their
military role, and gradually the *murabits* became *marabouts*.

But with the *ribat* of Sousse we are still in the heroic age of

Islam when the emphasis was martial. The building is a simple hollow square with towers at each corner and in the middle of each wall. One of the towers was a lookout and stands sixty feet above the roof. A single entrance leads to the courtyard, and round this square are two storeys of unconnected cells, storerooms, and an arsenal. A staircase leads from the courtyard to a gallery on the second floor, and off this is a prayer-room with a *mihrab*, or niche, pointing toward Mecca.

What makes such a building so exhilarating? The *ribat* is like a ship, with purpose and meaning in every part. But the excitement it arouses is greater than a simple pleasure in function and form. The shape of castles, fortresses, keeps, seems to satisfy an old craving—for security? for dangers not much greater than our strength? for a defensible position in a threatening world? The thick walls and round towers promise all this, and for a moment the threats and dangers shrink to manageable size. But there is more to the *ribat* than that. The architecture is massive and severe, like war and like the religion of early Islam. Yet it shares the cheerfulness of Sousse. One can imagine the *murabits* going about the routine of their day—on watch in the tower, exercising their horses outside the walls, practicing arms, praying before the *mihrab*, probing the Koran—happily. They were doing what they wanted to do and what they conceived to be their duty, sure that even if the walls of the *ribat* should fall, they would have their reward.

South of Sousse the landscape seems to expand; space grows greater and objects smaller; the hills flatten out and cede importance to the sky. Something in the air—dust or a breath from the sea—catches and reflects the light, blurring the outlines and softening the colours of distance. The coast is indented and muddled with sand bars and lagoons. Watery sheets of *sebkhas* lie between the olive groves. From the road you see a single palm tree that appears to be growing in the sea; you would not be surprised to see a boat push its way across the fields up to the road.

After several miles of this aqueous, equivocal landscape, you catch sight of the first of a string of little fortress towns that stand along this coast. Rising on promontories above the fields and *sebkhas*, they seem to be floating in air or resting on the breast of the sea. There is something familiar about them: no later accretions alter their medieval shape: the crenellated walls, the battlements, domes, and spire gleam through the luminous air as if through mists of time. You *remember* them, because all cities were once like this, isolated, coherent, discrete, built to the size of man. Each of them faces the sea like the capital of a city-state—a polis, not a megapolis.

The highway, with a modern prejudice for the shortest line between important points, bypasses these towns. But if you take the small tracks through the olives and *sebkhas*, and drive up to the walls, you find the distinction between the rural and the urban preserved. For there is nothing primitive or mean about these towns, except in philistine terms of electricity and plumbing. The design of the walls, of mosque, square, fountain, and housefront is sophisticated and knowing, underlined with a vestige of Rome or Byzance, and confirmed by time. The men wear gold-embroidered vests and pastel knee-breeches. The women are decently veiled in silk or the sheerest wool. These are bourgeoisie, not village farmers, though they have their fields and orchards outside the walls. Weavers, jewellers, shoemakers, merchants keep no hours, but, mixing their work and leisure, have more time for both. The people are friendly but aloof. These cities wear the slow, inward smile of sleepers.

One of these Gioconda towns is Monastir. Ruspina was the ancient name of the port. The modern name comes from a Christian monastery that stood next to the sea and was transformed by the Arabs to a *ribat*. The scalloped city walls date from the 9th century, though the two principal gates were "modernised" in 1269. The *ribat*, which now rises inside the city walls at the very edge of the sea, was also brought up to date in the 17th century. Monastir is still a holy town, and the devout of the *Sahel* come to be buried under its walls. The cemeteries spread their flat whitewashed gravestones along the shore, like sheets laid on the ground to dry.

In the forlorn hour just before dawn, the women of Monastir have a custom of going out to sit with the dead, who are thought to be especially lonely at that time. At the other end of the day, the men of Monastir walk hand in hand atop the ramparts to watch the sun go down and darkness come over the sea. Such habits have been passed from generation to generation, like the patterns of local embroidery or a variation in speech or dress that immediately spells Monastir to those that can read. The traditions and character of each town are preserved by the wide stretch of countryside between them, by the protecting walls, and by the attachment that makes each the centre of its people's world. Life in Monastir is undoubtedly confined, circumscribed, dull. But like *espalier* fruit rigorously pruned and trained to the sunny supporting wall, the flavour of existence is sweet and true. The light of all those habitual sunsets and dawns seems to have coloured the walls of Monastir, bathing the town in an amber liquor distilled of memory and time.

Mahdiya, said Ibn Khaldoun, is like a dagger held in a fist. It is built on a rocky peninsula, five hundred yards across at the base but thrusting a mile into the sea. During the Middle Ages and Renaissance, Mahdiya was known to European sailors and geographers simply as "Africa" and is so designated on maps today. The history of Mahdiya begins in the 9th century, when a Moslem missionary converted a tribe of Algerian Berbers to the Shi-ite branch of Islam, led them against the orthodox

Monastir—aerial view of La Keraya

ruler in Kairwan whom he replaced with a Fatimite prince—a descendant of the Prophet's daughter Fatima—who took the title *El Mahdi*, "The Directed One." Other Berbers counter-rebelled, and the Mahdi was forced to withdraw to this rocky peninsula, where he founded his capital of Mahdiya. The Mahdi's forces eventually recaptured Kairwan and all of North Africa, as well as Sicily. But for the Fatimites, the West was merely a springboard for pursuit of their claim to be Caliph of all Islam. With the wealth of Africa and Sicily and the support of their Berber adherents, they embarked from Mahdiya to the conquest of Egypt and Syria. The city of Cairo was founded in their honour and, in 973, they moved there, leaving a loyal Berber clan to rule Africa for them.

Though impregnable from land, the fortress of Mahdiya proved highly vulnerable from the sea. Twenty years after the departure of the Mahdi, the city was captured and largely destroyed by European crusader-pirates. In the 13th century it was occupied by Normans from Sicily, then liberated by Arabs from Morocco. The following century, French, English, and Genoese forces had a stab at it. It became the home port of the pirate Dragut, and in 1550 the troops of Charles V captured it and dismantled the walls before departing. Of late, Mahdiya has been a quietly prosperous fishing town, with a fleet of trawlers sheltering near the ancient port cut out of rock, and a row of thriving canneries stretching down the coast. If Mahdiya smiles behind the Dark Porch—a part of the old fortifications left standing on the land front—it may be in memory of a brilliant, if convulsive past.

Then the unexpected struck again. In 1907 a sponge diver found off the point of Mahdiya what he thought to be a submerged city—stacks of columns and cornices, blocks of cut and uncut stone, and heaps of broken pottery. Archaeologists came and found beneath this a floor of planks, and under that a compendium of Hellenistic furnishings and a few original Greek statues. The drowned city was in fact a Roman ship, returning with loot and ballast from Athens, that was wrecked off this coast in 81 B.C.

The sponge diver's catch is now in the museum of the Bardo in Tunis, where after their common experience—the abduction from Athens, the shipwreck and long submersion, and the dramatic rescue—they have the dazed look of lucky but battered survivors. Most are scarred by the experience, the bronzes roughened and eaten away with salt, the marbles broken, with one side discoloured like a sleeper's cheek from the pillow. Nails and planks from the ship itself and a pair of anchors are displayed like trophies. The furnishings reflect great refinement: the lines of a reconstructed bed have reached the utmost point of elegance; the horses' heads used as finials are prototypes of the velvet-eyed, nostril-quivering *houyhnhnms* of official art of the last century. One feels that the forms were already as familiar to the Greeks of the first century before Christ as they are to us today. They must have appealed to the culture-hungry Romans, as they confirmed the taste of 1907.

The sculpture is also in the genteel tradition. On some marble urns, the frenzy of maenads is reduced to a rhythmic swirl of drapery and counterpoint of crossed legs. Matching busts of Dionysus and Ariadne might be the same intermediate sex, not out of place on an Edwardian tennis court. Eros, a life-size bronze, is represented as a winged adolescent, *sec,* unseductive, a little smug. Statuettes of dancing dwarfs, one very male and one very female, are the dirty jokes of polite society. There is only one disturbing piece in the lot: a herm of Dionysus. Here the disturbance comes from the mixture of styles. The hair and beard are almost Assyrian in their rigidity; the short nose, deep-set eyes, and low brow are classically placid; the beret-like hat made of a flat coil of ribbons falls in Baroque convulsions; the phallus is just three crude blobs stuck to the front of the pillar. The work has been dated to the 2nd century B.C. Then why this mixture of archaic, classical, and advanced styles? Perhaps something in the cult of Dionysus suggested it, some unlimited potential of the god. The lips are parted as though about to speak, the empty eye sockets once glinted with ivory or enamel. It must have been a compelling image of the old adam lurking within the dandy. Yet the combination of hairiness and elegance was also Edwardian. In fact, Dionysus looks like the apotheosis of Edward VII.

We should be grateful to the Romans for collecting and copying Greek art instead of trying to replace it with something of their own. We may also be grateful to chance which decreed that the Roman ship would be wrecked 2000 years ago so that these relics would survive until now. Let us also be grateful to Mahdiya in whom the parted lips of a drowned god and the over-reaching gaze of the Directed One blend to create a rapt smile.

The first thing you notice about Sfax—the most important thing about Sfax—is the olive. Miles before you come to the city you enter the 'Forest of Olives', a huge semicircle of more than a million acres sweeping around the city from coast back to coast. There is no interruption, not a house nor a garden nor any other tree, for these are not farms but plantations. It is capitalism applied to agriculture, impressive but monotonous.

The trees are aligned like crosses in a military cemetery, in intersecting rows that stretch as far as the eye can see. Gone are the arthritic shapes, the exposed roots, the look of iron tenacity. Here each tree is a leafy balloon floating on a uniform, footed column. Even the colour seems less faded and evanescent, no longer "the hue of distance". The branches are powdered pale yellow with flowerets, or hung with bronze fruit each on the end of a little flexible twig like bunches of cherries. Each tree is endowed with its own demesne, seventy-five feet from its neighbours, where the roots can spread without competition and grow into another tree as round and perfect as the one above. The olive trees of Sfax are optimum, like the bodies of well-fed Americans.

Near the city you pass through a smaller semi-circular belt of almonds, pomegranates, aromatic plants and flowers, which Sfax puts to commercial use too. But still the olive is king: storehouses and presses crowd the road, and the air is lubricated with the heavy, sour smell of olive oil. Some of the oil of Sfax is pure and delicious, but the industry does not rely on the table alone. The stones are pressed again and again to obtain the thick, evil-smelling stuff that goes into soap, lubricants, and God knows what other miracles of science. The roads near the city are animated with bicycles, camels, trucks, donkeys, and people. At the presses, camels and trucks jostle anachronistically to deliver their loads. The fruit is placed in flat, beret-shaped mats woven in the villages, and then into imported machinery of dazzling modernity.

Sfax is pre-eminently an economic city. Let other towns be political or holy: Sfax is a producer. In ancient times she exported olive oil and woollen cloth throughout the Mediterranean. Stationary fisheries are staked out on the coastal shelf as systematically as the olive plantations. Boats from Greece and Sicily come in season for octopus and sponge. Tankers and freighters of all registrations pick up olive oil, salt, esparto grass, and especially phosphates, of which Tunisia is one of the world's top producers. The port has been enlarged since the War, and the depots, docks, and loading gear form a monumental suburb on the shore. The possibility of adding petroleum to the list of Sfax's exports has brought American and French exploration crews to the city.

With all this emphasis on economics, it is surprising to find the old city of Sfax the most beautiful in Tunisia. That English aesthete Ronald Firbank is said to have found it the most

Sfax—a market under the walls

beautiful city in the world. Perhaps it hits harder for being unexpected. I first saw Sfax when a great part of the new city was levelled with Allied bombings. It was a stormy day. The sky looked torn in two, and the wind raised the dust from the rubble of buildings as if they had just fallen. The old city reared back from this scene of devastation, impregnable and intact, as if it would outface the trump of doom.

Even on sunny days, Sfax is clothed in authority and power. The walls are like the base of a pyramid: the curtains appear to be leaning backwards and the octagonal towers are thickest at the base. The parapet is spiky with pointed merlons, and the upper walls pierced at intervals with embrasures for cannon. The magnificent Gate of the Diwan is actually a tunnel that turns a right angle in the deep course of the wall. Inside the walls, the density of houses seems greater even than that of Tunis, and the streets are heavy with sculptured doors and intricate *mesharabiyyas*. The beauties of Sfax date from many different periods: the walls were first built in the 9th century, though altered and faced with stone since; the Gate of the Diwan dates from 1306 and was restored in the 18th century; the Great Mosque is 10th century work, embellished ever since; some of the finest housefronts are of the 19th century. The style of Sfax has not relaxed or deteriorated. There is nothing soft or seductive. It is one with the rigorousness of the olive plantations, the rationale of the phosphate plants, the hard lure of gain that attracts Greek fishermen and American oil companies alike. The beauty of Sfax is the beauty of success.

VIII. THE *BLED*

"BLED" IS AN ARABIC WORD WITH A ROOT SIGNIFYING TO OCCUPY or settle. It is used therefore to mean "town", but with the Arabs' recognition of the co-immanence of opposites, it may also mean the country. In Tunisian parlance it is the equivalent of the backwoods. To live in the *bled* is to rusticate; a man from the *bled* is a yokel, a hick. I use the word here to designate the central portion of Tunisia, an undefined hinterland south of the *tell*, inland from the *sahel*, and north of the great *shotts*, or "shores", of the Sahara.

The guidebooks warn: "A monotonous region devoid of interest", and "No provisions along the way." Most of it is steppeland, a flat treeless heath that turns briefly green in spring, parched in summer, and bleak and windswept in winter. The sky is high and wide, but opaque, like a huge brazen bowl. The earth is scored by *wedds*, dry eroded gullies that fill suddenly with torrents in the rare rainfall and run wastefully into *sebkhas* or the sea. A lunar landscape: and appropriately the vegetation is chiefly of the genus *artemisia*— sagebrush and wormwood. There are a few lost settlements and withered farms, but it is a land of mere subsistence, neither desert nor sown. It is what nowhere must look like.

It is also the country of mirages. The sun and air play tricks on the eye all over Tunisia, but here in the half world of the *bled*, the illusory and the real seem to take each other's place in an endless charade. You drive by a glittering *sebkha* in the morning, and in the afternoon it is not there. On the horizon you notice a curious rock formation; the next time you pass, it is the ruins of a Berber village. As you look at a grove of stunted olives straggling along the bank of a *wedd*, they move and become a herd of camels casting black shadows in the sun. Those flat stones are the tents of nomads, and those birds feeding on the carcass of a goat are only stones. The brilliance of light and transparency of air fool the eye and mind into seeing things that are not there.

The absence of details makes distance deceptive too, as at sea or across a chasm. The roads run straight to the horizon like lines drawn on a map. There are no obstacles, no traffic, no dips or turns not visible far in advance. You press the accelerator and still have the impression of standing still on an empty plain. The horizon recedes ahead of you, and when you cross an occasional rise there seems always to be an identical road drawn across an identical plain beyond. Yet you can cross the whole region in one day.

In the middle of nowhere, an Arab appears ahead, walking steadily beside the road, wrapped in wool against the sun and carrying his shoes. Sometimes he will be riding a small donkey, both of them half asleep. Yet there is not a habitation in sight and no name on the map within thirty miles. Arabs are great travellers; when they can travel no other way, they walk. My carpenter who left Sidi-bou-Saïd for Mecca had to walk the length of this road, cross the Libyan desert and the width of Egypt, pass over Sinai and down the shore of the Red Sea. He may not be in Mecca yet. But all the lonely walkers in the *bled* are not going so far; probably only from one lost village to another, a mere day's walk. An hour between these horizons seems an eternity to us.

Some of these villages are marked on the road and a dirt track goes off at an angle and disappears in the *bled*. A few are near the road: mud-walled, the houses of unwhitewashed clay, the people dressed in earth-coloured *jebbahs* and blankets, as if the dust of the ground had just been breathed upon, and raised itself up into houses, walls, and men. You feel a really good rainstorm would wash them all back to primæval clay.

But the people most at home in the *bled* are the nomads. They move up and down these roads, northward in spring, to the south in winter. Sometimes it is just a single family, a man with two wives, a half-grown child or two, and a baby slung on one woman's back, the cattle consisting of one donkey and three or four goats. Others form a caravan that strings out half a mile and comprises fifty or sixty people of all ages, a dozen camels, several donkeys and horses, and a great mixed herd of sheep and goats. The humps of the camels are made twice as high with household gear—the black tents and red and orange rugs that make the nomads' house, huge copper pans and clay jars of water and oil; perched on top may be a sick woman or a baby tied on amidst the pots and pans. Sometimes the camels pull great two-wheeled carts painted orange and blue and piled with the same gear. Under the cart a fierce white kabyle dog trots chained to the axle. The horses are more often bony than fine, but saddles and bridles are bright with brass studs and coloured tassels. If the horse is white, his hooves and tail will be dipped in henna and a henna hand-print clapped on his rump against the evil eye. The donkeys have that look of great refinement, dove-grey and black, with delicate almond eyes and calyx ears and hooves like ebony slippers; and are subject to enormous loads of faggots or gear that leave only their feet and the tips of their ears visible. The goats are rusty black and scrawny; the sheep matted and earth-coloured, with heavy steatopygous tails that trail in the dust and give them a distressing waddle.

The bedouin are not a race: they represent a way of life. Some are blond or sandy haired, with freckles and grey eyes. Others are negroid, their black skins wrinkled and dusted grey with exposure. But a large proportion of the Tunisian bedouin have a pure semitic look. The men are tall and lean with deep-set eyes, high cheeks, and noses like hawks; their clothing is often ragged and the colour of dust, the basis of it a long cotton shirt, knee breeches with voluminous seats, a faded *chechia* bound with rags, and sometimes a burnous. The women can be strikingly beautiful, with fine features and luminous eyes; when they are young they walk like queens, but soon become hags bent double with work and rheumatism. The female costume never varies in form: it is like a Greek *chlamys*, made of a single strip of cotton, usually dark blue but sometimes yellow or red, which is wrapped round the hips, over the breasts and back, and pinned at the shoulder with heavy silver clasps, often revealing the profile of one naked breast. The women never veil, except in dust storms when they wrap their heads in shawls of brilliant aquamarine or watermelon pink. Their chins, cheeks, and foreheads are tattooed with abstract figures, and they are loaded with silver jewellery—bracelets, anklets, necklaces, brooches, head chains—which is the family bank account, accumulated in good years and sold when times are bad. The older children, dressed like miniatures of their parents, drive the herds or lead an animal on a string. The pubescent girls are ravishing. None of them, not even the smallest children, notice you as you drive past.

The caravans stop at wayside wells where the children water the cattle, and the women fill receptacles for the next day's march—goatskins or graceful clay amphorae, or most highly prized nowadays, a jerry-can left over from the war. Shortly before dark, they choose a camp site, often just a bare field near the road, and pitch their black tents. The women hunt brush-wood for fires; they have been gathering dung all day, as well as edible leaves and roots; and they settle down for the night. Sometimes you see the camp fires burning and hear the sound of flute and drum—a wedding or a circumcision party; but usually the tents are dark and look like part of the darkened earth, except for the gleam of a watchdog's eye. In hot weather, the caravans move at night and rest by day wherever they can find a bit of shade.

The bedouin are as remote and mysterious to the town Arab as the American Indian is to a resident of Manhattan. The townsmen speak of them in wonder, a little fear, and I suspect a large dash of ignorance. I was told that on his wedding night a bedu groom is expected to beat his wife unmercifully, and if he does not she may leave him. I was also told that bedu children stand in a circle round a woman in labour and watch their younger siblings brought into the world. Though nominally Moslem, the bedouin are thought by bourgeois Arabs to practise pagan rites and have pagan morals. I do not know the truth of any of these things. Some of the bedouin seemed to me to lead lives that were barely human. Others are rich in cattle, silver, and tribal grazing land, produce blankets and rugs of considerable beauty, and practise poetry and music. I felt nostalgia for their pastoral way of life, and envied their look of pride and freedom. And no people of such physical beauty can be looked down upon.

The freedom of the nomadic bedouin is, of course, the freedom of necessity, the only kind perhaps there is. The bedouin are on the move because they have to be, to pasture their flocks, to find seasonal work in the olive groves and wheat fields of the settled communities, and to hunt such wild crops as the esparto grass which they sell in town to be shipped to England to be made into fine paper. Many of them are part-time nomads, moving between summer and winter homes, but still driven by necessity. Their polygamy is another need: when a first wife is made old with wandering, work, and babies, a younger one is taken to help. The bedouin are increasing, because of this and because of modern medical care, and modern states consider them a problem. One solution is to make them settle as peasants, and a few tribes have successfully made the transformation. But others insist on remaining foot-loose. Habits can be necessities too.

Crossing one of the horizons and climbing an almost imperceptible wrinkle in the *bled*'s monotonous hide, you look on a plain darkened with patches of dusty olive trees and your eye is caught by a strange shape among them—the shape of a flat spool lying on one face. It would be pleasant to see it for the first time in ignorance, to have a sense of wonder and mystery, but in these well-documented times that pleasure is not possible. The spool-like object, you know in advance, is the amphitheatre of Thysdrus, now called El Jem. You lose sight of it as you descend the wrinkle and advance across the plain. Then, dramatically, it looms dead ahead, the road running straight up to the walls, then round them, like a thread winding round the spool. The effect, no matter how well informed you may be, is astonishing. On the north side there is nothing but a few olive trees, a drift of prickly pear and a couple of wretched *gourbis* to detract from the isolation and grandeur. It is not a beautiful structure—the usual birthday cake style, with three tiers of arcades and half columns, and traces of an unpierced upper storey decorated with pilasters; 120 feet high and 485 across. Not so big as the Colosseum; but the Colosseum is in Rome, and this is in the middle of the *bled*. The town of El Jem—a dusty warren of blind-faced hovels and dirt streets—is to the south, completely hidden by the mass of the amphitheatre. The present population is 5000; the seats of the amphitheatre held ten times that many. Thysdrus was a rich Roman colony, so rich that she was taxed heavily to finance one of those interminable Roman wars on the Danube and revolted. The Thysdrusites thereupon elected their own pro-consul Gordianus as Emperor; the Gordians were defeated, but the revolt spread and led eventually to the Emperor Maximian's downfall. It is pleasant to hear the echo of these old, important events in such a lost place as El Jem. The rest of ancient Thysdrus—the streets and houses and public buildings that must have spread round the amphitheatre—has disappeared. Another wry comment on Roman civilisation.

Today El Jem is a bedouin town. The caravan routes pass through and there are always encampments of nomads in the *bled* round about. Monday is market day, when villagers, peasants, and nomads gather in the shadow of the amphitheatre to buy, sell, and exchange their meagre goods and the brightly coloured excreta of industrial civilisation. A corral is set up for the exchange of livestock, and the inner man is enticed with cauldrons of frightful smelling messes and bloody sheep's heads lying on the ground. In a one-room *gourbi* under the amphitheatre walls a couple of local whores, heavily painted and covered with silver jewellery, set up shop.

Market day at El Jem is a pale shadow of the Roman holidays at Thysdrus (Gordianus was noted for the splendour of his games), just as the village is a ghost of the Roman city and the dusty olive trees wan descendants of the groves that supported the opulence of old. And this is part of the bedouins' story too. The prosperity of North Africa was proverbial in Punic and Roman times and extended well into the Moslem era. It did not dissipate gradually, either as a result of natural processes or, as is sometimes claimed, because of Arab indifference. It vanished suddenly and completely in the middle of the 11th century, four hundred years after the Arabs arrived. The cause was politics, and the bedouin were the instrument.

When the Mahdi's descendants moved to Cairo in 972, they left North Africa in the hands of their Berber vassals, the Zirides. For half a century the Zirides remained loyal lieutenants, but then they repudiated their allegiance to the Fatimites and recognised the orthodox Caliph of Baghdad. The infuriated rulers of Egypt punished their disloyal vassals in a diabolical way. Cairo had long been troubled by the lawless-

The Amphitheatre at El Jem

ness and rapacity of the nomadic tribes of upper Egypt. The Fatimites gave each of the tribes a sum of gold and promise of fair pillage and sent them into their former territories on promise they would never return to Egypt again.

Nomads had always existed in North Africa but since Roman times they had been held in check. The Hilalian invasion, as it is called from the name of the foremost tribe, was unprecedented. The Egyptian bedu swarmed to the west like human locusts, arriving in successive waves for more than a decade. They plundered farms and villages, burned orchards, and cut down the olive trees for fire wood. Their herds stripped the vines, trampled gardens, and devoured the fields of grain. The Zirides were forced to abandon their capital in Kairwan and take refuge on the spit of Mahdiya. The Government slipped into chaos. Cities and towns were isolated and at the mercy of the nomads. The roads were dangerous, and cultivation of outlying fields was abandoned. Worst of all, the irrigation systems that had taken centuries of Punic, Roman, and Arab skill to construct and maintain were damaged beyond repair. The vengeance of the Fatimites was thorough: they created a famine from which Tunisia has not recovered to this day. The bedouin who roam the *bled* are at home in a world their ancestors made.

Nothing is consistent with itself. There are farms in the *bled*. They require great courage and stamina, in plants as well as in men, and above all patience. Although the drought might seem eternal, a year would come at last when the rains were early and late in long drenching downpours that reached the deepest root. Then the almond tree would blossom in a pink cloud caught in black branches, and the olive hang out hundreds of little oval bronze balls; and the sheep fatten and the lambs live, and silver gleam again on the bedouin women's breasts. But the lean years outnumber the fat, and the farmers of the *bled* learn to live like the olive tree which stays alive on nothing by producing nothing, ready to bear when the good time comes.

One such farm belonged to the handsome Arab I had met at the Christmas party at Hammamet. Suddenly, just off the main road, you came upon a large yellow stone arch with no fence or wall on either side—a triumphal arch in the desert—and only a dirt track running through. Beyond was a grove of young olive trees, unexuberant and grey as lichen, and a few brittle almonds. The house was a touch of Hammamet in the *bled*, low and whitewashed, but the only shade came from a couple of pepper trees and a huge *caroub*. On the steps an old pointer bitch lay in the sun, and around a corner would come Hassan, as like as not a shotgun in his arms, with a smile of welcome on his perfect features.

Hassan was in his thirties when I first knew him. He was the son of an old, rich family of Tunis, and as a young man had travelled widely in Europe, the Near East, and the United States. He was at home in any society and spoke English and French with polished perfection. A few years ago he had re-tired to this property in the *bled*. He lived alone, except for one servant and the old bird dog; but he had a much adored daughter of eight or nine who was being brought up by his family in Tunis. He seldom left the farm, except for business in Tunis or the *Sahel*, or to see his daughter. After months of absence, he would appear unannounced at Hammamet or Sidi-bou-Saïd, to stay a few minutes or a few days as the fancy struck him, then vanish again into the *bled*. Laila adored him, and when I teased her about this she said, "But he is my son too", though they were nearly the same age.

If I insist on Hassan's physical beauty it is because I think it is a moral quality, the way great wealth or poverty or a physical deformity may be. I am not sure whether it is a blessing or a curse, but people who have it are set apart from the rest of us. First of all they have enormous power, uncon-

nected with accommodation, wit, or winning ways; and this
is a danger for themselves as well as others. Then there is the
sadness that always accompanies beauty, the sorrow of things
that hold in beauty but a little moment, the disappointment of
promises unfulfilled. The early power, the easy road, the barriers flattened by the cosmic ray of their eyes have led to—
what? Neither the green gardens of Hammamet nor the dead
wastes of the desert. They have led into the *bled*.

Like most melancholy people, Hassan was a gay and charming companion. When I was a bachelor we sometimes spent
an evening together in the cafés of La Marsa or the night clubs
of Tunis. The hostesses approached us with glassy *bonhomie*
but under Hassan's brown gaze their glaze would melt and their
hearts begin to beat again for the first time in many years. He
was also a generous friend. I had seen a *slougui* on a desert trip
and longed to own one. These are the oldest domesticated
breed of dog, the prototype of canine beauty with pointed
muzzle and flat head, a long arched neck, deep chest, narrow
loins, strong nervous legs, and a tapered tail arched high over
the back. They are used in the desert to hunt gazelle and have
the speed and grace of their prey. They were rare and hard to
come by, and I had no luck in my search for one. I mentioned
it to Hassan—and a few weeks afterwards I came home to
find a beautiful, savage puppy, sand coloured with black
muzzle and points. I named him Targui, the singular of Tuareg,
for he reminded me of the veiled, kohl-painted warriors of
the Sahara.

Hassan's house in the *bled* was practically unfurnished except
for bits of Roman Thysdrus turned up in the fields by his
ploughmen. One of these was a bronze hand holding an olive
between thumb and forefinger in a gesture of benediction.
The garden had a similar air of incompleteness, like a fountain
gone dry. In the centre was a long sunken pool into which
water was meant to flow down the fluted side of an old pilaster.

But there was no water. Drought had gripped the *bled* for three years, and the garden blossomed only with Roman stones. In the orchard the almond trees and olives held on but bore no fruit, oblivious to the gesture of the bronze hand.

Our visits to Hassan all had this suspended quality. In the daytime we shot bustards out on the *bled* or tiny thrush among the olive trees; the latter were served for dinner in holocausts, each on a bier of toast, with their last meal of olives still in their little guts, and eaten whole, bones, stuffing, and all except for the skull and thigh. At night we sat on cushions round the fireplace, or around the empty garden pool under the wide grey sky. Hassan was one of the few educated Arabs I knew who knew and admired the bedouin. He let them camp on his land and use his well; and he had an olive press where they were free to make their own oil. They in turn accepted him in their encampments. He could sing their songs, and he translated their poetry into French verse. We asked him to take us to visit a nomad camp, and one weekend when we were staying with him we went to a bedouin wedding.

Another couple went with us, friends and neighbours from Sidi-bou-Saïd. The husband was an Arab, the wife French; they were both doctors, worked long and hard hours in Tunis, had three children and a large haphazard house near ours. Ali, the husband, was grave, soft-spoken, and withdrawn, until suddenly his fancy or his sympathy was struck and gave out sparks. Francine was volatile, impatient, outspoken, and generous. They were happy, quarrelsome, and devoted.

The five of us piled into Hassan's jeep and set out, first on the main road, then on a dirt track that was clearly not designed for motor traffic, and finally across the unmarked *bled*, arriving somewhat shaken at the nomads' camp. Why they had chosen this particular piece of emptiness was hard to say. Two groups of tents about a hundred yards apart rose from the ground like ranges of low hills. A single tent stood apart, and there the bridegroom waited for us alone. He wore a new *burnous* and had the semitic features and bold look of a true Hilalian. As friends of Hassan's we were greeted with grave courtesy and invited into the tent. A brisk wind whipped over the *bled*, but the tent was reinforced with hot-coloured blankets on the windward side, and the ground was covered with more layers of wool. We sat cross legged in a circle, and the bridegroom served us glasses of piping hot, clear, sweet mint tea.

Soon another young man appeared outside the tent with a large steaming bowl which the bridegroom took from him and set before us on the rugs. It was a *couscous*, but a kind I had never seen before. The meat was one great chunk of white lard—the tail of a fat-tailed sheep. Francine and my wife exchanged a look of horror.

Hassan said in English, "This is a great honour. That is the fat ration for the whole clan for at least a month."

Our host reached into the bowl and broke off chunks of solid fat in his fingers, placing them before us. "*Bismillah*" we murmured politely. The two women turned pleading eyes to Hassan.

"You can't hurt his feelings," Hassan said heartlessly, and Ali added, "Go ahead—eat it."

The bridegroom did not sit with us, but busied himself serving us bread and tea. I took a small bit and, trying not to think of the rear view of a Tunisian sheep, swallowed it whole. "It's no worse than your first oyster," I said. My wife does not eat oysters.

While the bridegroom's back was turned, Francine shoved her portion in front of her husband. "It's your country," she muttered. My wife quickly put hers back into the common bowl.

Our host was delighted with our appetites. He reached into the pot and broke off more of the tail, ignoring our protests as mere politeness. Francine gulped down her glass of boiling hot tea and when the bedouin turned away to fill it the three of us disposed of the fat where we could. Ali and Hassan ate heartily and laughed at our distress.

The bridegroom served us a third time. At last Hassan took pity: "Leave it in front of you. He thinks you're still hungry."

"Isn't that rude?" my wife asked.

"It means you've had enough. He'll have to kill another sheep if you keep on eating. Don't worry—there are lots of people in the tents who will eat what we leave."

We left the fat untouched before us. The host cheerfully put it back in the bowl and took the *couscous* away.

Francine and my wife asked to see the bride, and the bridegroom led them across the field to a group of tents. They came back in quarter of an hour, infected with wedding hysteria. The bedouin women had examined them both minutely with anthropological interest, touching, prodding, and inspecting them down to their underwear. They congratulated Francine on her three children and commiserated with my wife for having none. The bride was an exquisite child of twelve or thirteen. My wife gave her a brooch she was wearing, and the little girl kissed her on the shoulders and breast in thanks.

A shot rang out. Then the piercing *ou-lou-lou-lou* that Arab women make with their tongues in celebration or war was carried by the wind over the field. A group of men emerged from one range of tents, a group of women from the other. One man rushed into the field. He leapt into the air and stamped his feet on the ground. In his hands he brandished a shotgun; another shot split the air, and the earth spat between the groups.

Among the warbling women a shape heaved upward—it was a camel, its hump crowned with a figure entirely swathed in dark-coloured stuffs. The women fled across the field clutching the trappings of the camel protectively, chased by

A Berber horseman in wedding attire

the men from the other tents. The women veered and doubled back, the figure on the camel swaying dangerously as the animal swerved. At last the men caught them and took the camel and its burden away. Shots of jubilation were fired in the air.

The bride had been captured. The wedding was over.

Amused and even excited by the mock abduction, we were preparing to leave when a band of horsemen dashed from beyond the tents across the field. They spurred their horses full speed towards us, and reined them sharply or veered just before crashing into the tent. Then they began a complicated gavotte, galloping round the field, changing direction, man-œuvring in wild measures. The riders shouted in short, sharp syllables, and the women set up their bird-like *ou-lou-lou-lou* again. As we watched, the horsemen formed in two lines at opposite sides of the field. Then the two lines galloped head on toward each other. We held our breath as they approached, but the lines passed through each other, still at full speed, like the teeth of two combs. At the edges of the field, they turned, formed again, and repeated the manœuvre. This was dangerous stuff. Each line of horsemen rode stirrup to stirrup, flank to flank, but the two lines met, intermingled, and passed on, avoiding collision by some miracle of precision and skill.

Then something happened. The fifth or sixth time, a horse stumbled or veered—I don't know what—and two of them met head on. We could hear a clap, like two pieces of wood, as their skulls collided. One horse staggered across the field, his rider still clinging to his back. The other dropped and lay twitching on the ground. His rider was thrown into the air and sprawled still where he fell, as if he had been dropped from the sky. Hassan and Ali rushed toward him, and the other men ran across the field.

I held back with Francine and my wife and waited. The *ou-lou-lou* of the women stopped abruptly. Then from one of the tents came a new sound, of wailing. A group of women came slowly across the field. One of them, no doubt the wife of the fallen rider, lay back against the others, her arms pinioned out by her companions, her feet dragging, propelled by the others toward the accident. As she approached we saw her face raised to the sky in a mask of grief. Facing her, another woman walked backwards, a knotted thong in her hands. With the thong, she was lashing the stricken woman across the face.

Have I mentioned the rain in Tunisia? North Africa has been called a cold country with a hot sun; it might also be described as a dry country with torrential rains. The rain does not come often, but when it does, the water streams from the sky violently, without measure, as if intending another Babylonian deluge. At least once a year the streets of Tunis are flooded, gutters streaming, squares turned into ponds, ground floors awash with water and mud. Traffic is stranded, and the electricity fails. In the country, the earthen walls of *tabias* cave in and the mud villages begin to dissolve. The rain does not soak into the ground; the sun-baked soil cannot drink it fast enough, and the water rushes along the surface, seeking the tortuous *wedds*, and running wastefully into the sea. The bedouin go to the highest ground and huddle in their tents; when it is over you see the fields spread with drying rugs and blankets and strips of blue cloth. No wonder they are bent over with rheumatism. But the *wedds* are dangerous. Dry as dust most of the year, they become large swift rivers, filling so suddenly that whole caravans are swept away, and the bodies of men, camels, sheep, and goats are found jumbled in the mud of a *sebkha* or floating on the edge of the sea.

My wife and I were driving through the *bled* one evening when the sky opened and the rain came pelting down. The first *wedd* we came to was a sheet of water sweeping across the road from high ground on one side to fall over a ledge on the other. A line of cars waited on both sides. A truck drove up and decided to risk it; the water reached only to the hubcaps, so the cars followed.

We drove on a few miles till we came to a dip in the road itself, filled now with a swift brown stream. There were no other cars this time, but a bedu, bare-foot and with hoisted clothing, walked into the beam of my headlights.

"How deep?" I asked him.

He pointed to his leg just above the knee: "Follow me."

The bedu walked into the stream, feeling ahead with a staff. If I looked at the water, its flow seemed to pull us to the edge of the road, so I kept my eyes on the bedouin's back. In mid-stream the water swirled round his thighs but then began to sink as he moved up the other bank. I gave him a coin.

By now it was quite dark and the rain still fell. We were feeling the strain and beginning to long for a drink in front of the fire. There were more *wedds* ahead of us, but as many behind, and we had managed to ford them all so far. When we reached the next one, there were no other cars, and no bedu appeared out of the dark to help us.

I remembered this *wedd* when it was dry. It was broad but not very deep, and from the road you could glimpse the sea. What I did not know was that it flowed from hills where a particularly viscous clay, used by the local potters, was found. "St. Christopher, help us," I said, and drove in.

We had gone only a few feet when the wheels began to slip on the slimey surface of the road. I shifted to reverse, but it was already too late. We slid into the middle of the stream and stopped. The water reached halfway up the doors. Slowly the rear end of the car began to turn with the current till we were at right angles to the road, facing upstream. I raced the motor and heard it gasp like a drowning man. The hood sank beneath the water; the headlights shone amber for a moment and went out. We began to float gently backwards toward the sea.

My wife said, "I'm getting out."

"No you're not," I said. "You'd be swept away."

"What are we going to do?" she asked.

"I don't know. Pray."

The water began to seep under the doors and over our feet. I had no plan and tried to think of the best thing to do. Perhaps our car would snag on a sand bar or submerged tree. If turned over or drifted too near the sea, it would be time enough to swim for it. I do not know whether a drowning man really reviews his whole life. I know that I thought only of the present, not of the danger we were in only, but of our whole situation—my wife was pregnant for the first time—and of my happiness and—not in fear or anger, but ironically and a little sadly—of the end. There was a bottle of whisky in my bag, and I almost got it out for a farewell drink.

We had now drifted out of sight of the road. Suddenly a light flashed from the bank. I lowered a window.

"Who are you?" A man's voice, in French, reached us faintly through the sound of rain and the rushing stream.

"My wife is pregnant," I shouted back somewhat inconsequentially. "Have you got a rope."

The light wavered and went out.

"I think we've stopped moving," my wife said.

"Yes. We're stuck on something. We're all right now." She squeezed my hand, appreciating the assurance but not believing it. The water in the car was now up to our knees. We waited for what seemed a long time.

Out of the dark a pale form appeared. It was a man, stripped to his skin, waist deep in water. "Take this," he said, handing the end of a rope through the window. "It's tied to a tree."

I recognised him as a young *colon* I had met but hardly knew. I tied the rope to the shaft of the steering wheel. We pushed the door open and the water rushed in over our laps.

The Frenchman grasped my wife round the waist and disappeared with her in the dark. I waited till I saw a light flash on the bank. Then I untied the rope, wrapped it round my arm, and slid out of the car. My feet slipped in the mud and I was swept off by the current, but I gripped the rope and hand over hand I reached the bank. It was greasy and spiked with aloes. The young *colon* reached down and dragged me up.

"Why are you here?" I asked him as he put on his clothes.

"I was expecting someone from Tunis. I saw your lights on the road and thought it might be them." He looked at his watch. "They won't come now."

He took us to his house, gave us dry clothes, fed us, and let us spend the night. In the morning the sky had cleared, and we went to look at the *wedd*. It was still running sluggishly, thick with clay. My car had come adrift again and had floated further downstream. We found it turned on its side and half buried in a mud bank a few yards from the shore.

"Good thing you weren't in it," said the Frenchman. "Last time this happened a neighbour of mine was caught. His car turned over on him and trapped him in the mud. It was two days before we dug the body out."

IX. KAIRWAN

THE CITY OF KAIRWAN HAS NO NEIGHBOURS. IT STANDS ALONE, surrounded by the *bled*. Midway between sea and mountains, it is beyond the influence of both. The massive ochre walls rise straight from the featureless plain; above them swell the domes of a hundred mosques, and the sky is stabbed with the virile shape of minarets. A suburb of turban-shaped tombstones crowds beneath the walls, and herds of hobbled camels lurch across the prairie looking for grass. In isolation, Kairwan preserves its purity. As the shadow of night sweeps over the *bled* and the mountains of the Maghreb darken in the distance, a *muezzin* climbs the minaret of the Great Mosque and calls out over city and plain the pure, cold formula: *There is no god but God.* A caravan of pilgrims, perhaps carrying a corpse to be buried in holy ground, hurries to reach the city before dark. As the voice of the *muezzin* dies, the gates in the ramparts close.

When Sidi Oqba ibn Nafi arrived here only forty years after the Prophet's death, there was nothing but desert. Where he stopped, a spring of water broke miraculously from the ground at his feet. Stooping to drink, he picked out of the water a gold cup he had lost years ago in the holy fountain of Zem-zem in Mecca. On this sign, he pitched his camp and founded the city. Kairwan—the name means caravanserai—remains the most Arab town in Tunisia. There was no Punic, Roman, or Berber settlement here before, and nothing of importance was added by the Turks or the French. It was the base for the

Moslem conquest of the West, and the capital of Ifriqiyah for most of the five centuries of Arab rule. The inhabitants claim to be of pure Arab lineage. And it is one of the holiest cities of Islam.

North African Moslems believe that four—or seven, or nine (the number varies)—visits to Kairwan equal the required *hajj* to Mecca. I was a pilgrim many times over. The unique, uncompromising character of Kairwan pleased me, though it offended others. The streets are muddy and full of filth. The stench is frightful: you must do as the inhabitants do, buy a spray of jasmine heads threaded on pine needles and carry it under your nose. The flies crawl impartially from the dung heaps, across the skinned and gutted sheep hung on hooks and the organs piled on the counters, and into your eyes. Whole sections of the city are uninhabited, streets empty and houses falling in ruin. Rome must have looked like this in the Dark Ages.

One of the attractions of Kairwan is the rug industry. The rugs come in many patterns and colours, but the best and most original are in small, mosaic-like designs, made without dyes in wool the colours the sheep come in—brown, beige, cream, white, *tête-de-nègre*, grey, and black. They are woven by women in their homes and hawked in the streets by a native form of auctioneering it would be perilous for a foreigner to get involved in. In the shops the merchants say grandly, "We do not bargain here" and blandly ask for three times the rug's value. They offer you cups of coffee or tea, but I suspected they spat in my footsteps when I left. The people of Kairwan are arrogant as only possessors of the flame can be—in Rome or Boston or Mecca—when holiness becomes a private possession soiled by the familiarity of generations.

The other attraction of Kairwan is the mosques. To the perhaps parochial Moslems of North Africa, the sanctity of Kairwan is second only to Mecca among all cities of the world.

The wealthy have endowed the religious foundations and enriched the shrines with gifts of tiles, rugs, banners, and ornaments of all kinds, from rare manuscripts of the Koran to jewelled ostrich eggs and silver wedding dresses. The most devout come here to die or direct that their bodies be laid in a cemetery under the walls. The pilgrims arrive on foot, by camel and horseback, in ramshackle buses or crowded taxis, a few in limousines driven by liveried chauffeurs. They pitch their tents outside the walls, or stay at a *fondouk*—a hollow square of unfurnished cells for the people, round a big courtyard for their animals—or in a hospice attached to one of the mosques, or in one of many hotels. They visit each shrine and mosque and honour the saint or hero buried there. They drink water from the Well of Barouta that flows from Mecca. They squeeze between two pillars that winnow out the fat and self-indulgent from the portals of paradise. They gaze on the tomb of the Barber, which contains three hairs from Muhammad's beard.

For tourists, the procedure is cut and dried. You buy a ticket from the tourist office and are obliged to take a licensed guide. The mosques may be visited only at certain hours (between prayers) and the itinerary is always the same. One of the guides was old and angular, with one eye blotted out by trachoma, and a concave chest that made him rasp and wheeze. He was always accompanied by a swarm of flies that buzzed round his head when he walked and settled on his shoulders when he stopped. He was a true Kairwanese—"*pur sang arabe*" he said as if he were at stud—and threw the names and dates of conquests and dynasties, shrines and schisms at us, contemptuous of our ignorance of the capital of the world. He was also doubtless in collusion with the rug shops where every tour ended. I got fond of him, contempt, flies, villainy, and all, and asked for him every time until he died of whatever was gnawing inside his chest.

First, the Mosque of the Sabres, less than a century old but already a favourite with the simpler pilgrims and the simple-minded tourists. Sidi Amor, the *marabout* who built it, was a blacksmith and something of a clown. He filled the mosque with gigantic furniture, fashioned by himself: a huge pipe wreathed with meaningless inscriptions (was he illiterate?), a sword stuck fast in its scabbard which each tourist is asked to try to pull. In the courtyard lie some heavy anchors brought by Sidi Amor from Porta Farina against the day Kairwan becomes a seaport. There are five tombs, in three of which lie the bones of Sidi Amor, his daughter, and a servant. The others are reserved for the final *imam* and a companion. This *imam* will draw the sword from the scabbard, complete the seventh dome of the mosque which is now open to the sky, and save Islam. Blue-grey pigeons wheel through the hole of the seventh dome and perch on the waiting tombs, and the beat of their wings resounds through the mosque like the sound of subdued laughter.

The next stop is the Mosque of the Three Doors: no legends, but a handsome 9th century façade inscribed with arabesques, which was taken apart for the inclusion of a minaret in 1440 and put back stone by stone. Next, the Mosque of the Barber, which is what—the guide scolds us crossly—the ignorant insist on calling the tomb of Sidi Sahib, a companion of the Prophet who was buried with his most prized possession, three hairs from Muhammad's beard. The mosque stands outside the walls and looks like a miniature town itself, for a school, a hospice, retreat house, and various other connected buildings have grown up around it. Although the Prophet's Companion must have died in the 7th century, his shrine was refurbished in the 17th and has a rose-coloured minaret, doors of Italian marble, and a vestibule in cool blue-green tiles and white stucco. The whole is about as religious in feeling as the Petit Trianon.

Why, I used to wonder, were the mosques in Kairwan the only mosques in Tunisia open to the infidel? Every Tunisian I asked had a different answer. That the mosques of Kairwan were profaned by the invading French army in 1881 and therefore no longer holy. That sacrileges had been committed elsewhere, but not here, so the mosques in other places were henceforth closed to non-Moslems. That the Kairwanese care only for money and gladly prostitute their shrines to attract tourists. Listening to the scornful old guide, I wondered if this were not the ultimate arrogance of Kairwan. Elsewhere we were physically excluded from the mystery. Here the barriers are down; we are permitted to share the holiness, enter it, stare at it, even touch it. And we expect a revelation. Is this it—the miraculous well, the huge sword and pipe, the winnowing pillars, the whiskers of the Prophet? The single eye of the guide glittered with mockery. You thought you were admitted to the mystery? Fools! You will not find it here.

Where then is the mystery to be found? Islam is perhaps the most historical of the world's great religions, linked as it is with the history of a certain people in a certain country at a certain time. Mecca is inaccessible. Perhaps the history of Kairwan, itself an important chapter in the history of Islam, will provide a clue.

Apart from the resemblance to Arabia symbolised by the gold cup, the site of Kairwan had several practical advantages when Sidi Oqba arrived there from the sands of Libya in A.D. 670. The Arabs faced two enemies, the Byzantines and the Berbers. The unprepossessing site was out of reach of the Byzantine fleet on the coast, and it commanded the mountains where the Berber forces lodged. It was also near the intersection of the main caravan routes, both to the north and to the west. The Berbers at first welcomed the new invaders against the Byzantines, and many joined the ranks of Islam. But Sidi Oqba treated them as a subject people, even when they were converted, and severely punished any who apostasised. The Berbers thereupon repudiated the alliance and began fighting the invaders, alone or in conjunction with the Byzantines. The Arab Governor of Egypt, displeased with the results of Oqba's policy, sent his freedman Dinar to relieve him. Dinar took Oqba prisoner and abandoned Kairwan. He made peace with the great Berber chief Kusaila and was therefore able to occupy the country as far westward as Tlemsin.

Ten years later Sidi Oqba was reinstated by the Caliph himself. He threw Dinar in chains and re-established his old base at Kairwan. Kusaila quickly deserted the Arabs and withdrew into the mountains. Leading Dinar in chains, Oqba pushed westward across Africa till he reached the Atlantic. There, according to Moslem tradition, he rode his horse into the waves, declaring he would conquer the sea itself and the lands beyond for the One God. Turning back through what he thought was conquered territory, Sidi Oqba was attacked by Berbers near Biskra. He released Dinar from his chains and gave him a sword. Throwing their scabbards away, the two rivals fought side by side till they were cut down. The death of Oqba signalled a general uprising in which Berbers and Byzantines combined to throw the Arabs back into Libya. Kairwan was lost and Kusaila became master of the interior.

All of Sidi Oqba's conquests had to be won again by others. In 688 Kairwan was recaptured and Kusaila defeated and killed. Nine years later Byzantine power in Africa was broken when the Arabs took Carthage and defeated the Greek fleet. The Berbers continued resistance for a time; but by skilful diplomacy some of the tribes were regained for Islam, the rest defeated, and the pacification of Africa began.

Despite setbacks and dissension, the Arabs conquered Africa with the speed and ease of a sharp blade cutting through soft, ripe cheese. Perhaps the ripeness was all. Two centuries of invasion, the Vandal incursion and the Byzantine restoration, the dissatisfaction of the tribes, religious dissension and economic grief—all contributed to the softening. The Berbers, after their shortlived resistance, flocked to the standard of the invaders. The Arabs' roving, martial life and tribal organisation were similar to theirs, and no doubt the prospect of further conquest to the west appealed to them. But Islam itself must have been an attraction: it was simple and manly, and it sanctified many of their own basic instincts. The spread of Islam is sometimes ascribed to an Arab policy of conversion or death, circumcision by the sword as it were. If this were so we would expect to hear the name of at least a handful of Christian martyrs in 7th century Africa, for it is not human nature to submit to such an ultimatum. But the Arab invasion produced no Perpetua and Felicity, no Cyprian, not even a defiant Tertullian. The Arabs did not seek wholesale conversions. They considered themselves an hereditary élite, distinguished by blood and religion from their subjects. Although the religion of Jews and Christian was respected, a special tax was levied on non-Moslems, and mass conversion deprived the Arabs of revenue. Yet within a century Christianity vanished from North Africa, partly through flight but largely through voluntary submission to Islam. Perhaps the Africans thought: the cheese is ripe to rottenness.

But what of the blade? Sidi Oqba is enshrined at Kairwan as Allah's chief instrument in the westward advance of Islam. I am inclined to agree. That dash into the sea shows of what steel Sidi Oqba was made. He was of that breed who would conquer in any name—Christ's, Helen's, Marx'—and with such leaders the Arabs might have reached the Atlantic even if the angel Gabriel had never appeared on the coast of the Red Sea. Sidi Oqba was the sword of Islam, and Islam was a sword in his hand.

Perhaps his greatest single achievement was the founding of Kairwan. This was one of those momentous acts that alter the direction of history—acts which in religious terms may be ascribed to the Will of God. The establishment of a permanent base in Africa meant that the Arabs would no longer merely raid the Maghreb and then withdraw, that they were committed to remain in the West and—these things having a momentum of their own—to continue westward to Algeria, Morocco, and Spain, until the momentum died in southern Gaul. And by breaking new ground and ignoring the older centres, Sidi Oqba cut the history of Ifriqiyah in two as if with the edge of his blade. Carthage was the past : Kairwan the future. There was to be no dilution of the new with the old. The contending voices of the past were silenced by the cry of the muezzin : *There is no god but God. Muhammad is the messenger of God.*

The 9th century was the golden age of Kairwan. In 800, Ibrahim bin Aghlab, an Arab from Algeria, seized the city and thereby half of North Africa. The Aghlabite dynasty constructed an extensive irrigation system that brought water from the mountains to encircle the city in a green belt of parks and gardens. Aghlabite princes built the Great Mosque in its present form and erected and endowed the *ribats* along the coast. Under them, African religious thought and jurisprudence developed distinctive forms. The princes lived outside the walls of Kairwan, in a fortified palace set in gardens and guarded by an army of Negro slaves. Despite their patronage of religion, the Aghlabites themselves were said to live dissolute lives and indulge in the drinking of wine. Ambassadors from Charlemagne and renegade Byzantines were received at court. Kairwan's only rival for brilliance in the West was Cordova in Moslem Spain.

It was under the Aghlabites that the Arabs began the conquest of Malta, Sicily, and southern Italy. A Byzantine official, on the outs with the authorities of Syracuse, came to Kairwan seeking support. The seventy-year-old Qadhi of Kairwan was so enthusiastic for a crusade against the Christians that he led the first expedition himself. An army of 11,000 Arabs and Berbers sailed for Sicily. They laid seige to Syracuse, but an epidemic killed many of them, including the aged Qadhi. Joining forces with a body of Spanish Moslems arrived on a raid of their own, the survivors proceeded to reduce the island, city by city. Even before they controlled all of Sicily, they invaded the mainland—again invited by a Christian, the Duke of Naples who, in return for their help against the Duke of Benevento, helped the Moslems capture Messina. The victorious Africans pushed up the Adriatic, reduced Bari, and raided the territories of Venice.

In 846, an Aghlabite fleet appeared off Ostia. The Moslems sacked Rome outside the walls and seized the treasures of St. Peter and St. Paul, though the departing ships were destroyed by a storm. A few years later, the Arabs directed another raid toward Rome, but this time a Christian storm intervened first and destroyed the fleet before it got there—as can be seen in Raphael's frescos in the Stanze of the Vatican. The Franks and Byzantines finally drove them from central Italy, but Bari remained Moslem for thirty years, ruled at the end by an independent Sultan. And Sicily settled down to its most brilliant century as a province of Islam.

When the successors to the Aghlabites, the Fatimite princes, moved to Cairo in 972 they left an Arab dynasty to represent them in Sicily and a Berber clan, the Zirides, to rule in Kairwan. The city reflected an afterglow of the preceding centuries, and the countryside was prosperous. The Zirides collected taxes in the name of the Fatimites and forwarded part of the revenue to Cairo; and dutifully mentioned the Shi-ite Caliph in the public prayers. But most of the populace was not Shi-ite, and it may have occurred to the Zirides to wonder why the wealth of Ifriqiyah should be shared with Cairo. In 1049 the Ziride princes stopped payments to Egypt and substituted the name of the orthodox Caliph of Baghdad in the prayers.

We have seen what the wrath of the Fatimites unleashed in the *bled*. In six years the Beni Hilal reduced the plain of Kairwan to the desert that Sidi Oqba had found there and which exists today. The city became untenable. Simultaneously, Pisan and Genoese fleets attacked the coast. For the next two hundred years Ifriqiyah was fought for and dismembered by foreign and native adventurers. Tunis and Sfax became independent amirates. The Normans of Sicily occupied the cities of the *Sahel*. An Armenian *condottiere* named Karakoush tried to carve out a kingdom in the south. Berbers from Morocco and Spain fought each other for control of the country. At last a Moroccan named Abu Hafez quelled the chaos in the 13th century and established a dynasty that ruled for 350 years. But the Hafsite capital was Tunis. Kairwan had entered its dark age.

The holiness remains. There is one more monument to visit, and the guide always leaves it till last. It is the Great Mosque of Kairwan, the shrine of Sidi Oqba himself. It stands in one of the atrophied quarters of town, among empty streets and abandoned houses. The outside is like a fortress, with sloping walls and heavy buttresses blunted with layers of chalky lime. A squat tower of ochre brick stands at one end, and some dwarfish domes peer over the parapet. The impression is one of strength—severe, uncouth, almost brutal. Stepping through the gate you enter a wide flat courtyard with colonnades on three sides, a porch on the other. Behind the porch is a prayer-room, a vast hall supported by rows of columns. On the opposite side of the court stands the square tower, with two whitewashed balconies and cupola, to serve as a minaret. It is as simple and plain as that.

The Mosque of Sidi Oqba is the oldest Moslem edifice in

the West, parts of it perhaps the oldest in the world. Where
Sidi Oqba himself worshipped—if he prayed indoors at all—
is of course lost. This is the fifth or sixth mosque on the site,
erected by the Aghlabites and restored and embellished many
times since. But the form is as old as Islam: it follows the
design of the one built in Medina for Muhammad himself,
though greatly enlarged and translated from clay and palm
trunks into marble and stone. The building breathes the spirit
of primitive Islam. Sidi Oqba and his band were hard-headed
men of action, unlettered warriors recently emerged from the
Arabian desert, who had surrendered to the Will of God, but
to no other. Their city was a camp, their place of worship a
fortress. Later Islam might refine itself to the delicacy of the
Blue Mosque or the frivolity of the shrine of Sidi Sahib, and
Persian mysticism would some day inspire those eastern
minarets that seem to be suspended from the sky rather than
to rise from the earth. The minaret of Sidi Oqba is as earth-
bound as a mountain, its bricks dug from the earth, its single
door as low as the mouth of a cave. Its purpose was simply
that of a platform—to enable the *muezzin* to be heard
over the city, not to bring him closer to heaven. The
early Moslems submitted to God, they did not aspire to be
like Him.

Yet, as you look more closely as the Mosque of Sidi Oqba,
you see that the fabric itself is not all that simple. The walls
are a patchwork of brick and stone, augmented with blocks of
marble, even Latin inscriptions set sideways or upside-down.
The door of the minaret is framed with three antique lintels
carved with stylised foliage; the steps of the tower are made of
ancient grave stones. And the columns—both those that ring
the courtyard and those that throng the prayer-room—are a
heterogenous collection of ancient and medieval styles, of
marble, porphyry, and onyx, compiled from pagan temples,
Roman theatres, Vandal palaces, Byzantine basilicas, brought

Kairwan—minaret and courtyard of the Great Mosque

from the ruins of Hadrumetum, Thysdrus, Ruspina, and Carthage, mutilated, mismated, and indiscriminately combined. Yet the effect is neither classical, Christian, nor heteroclite. The Mosque is harmonious and unmistakably Arab, demonstrating that space, not wood or brick or stone, is the material of architecture.

The Mosque of Sidi Oqba was thrown up, of whatever materials lay at hand, in the rush of an urgent Idea. That Idea is the central conviction of Islam. Here is no pantheon of minor gods, no hierarchy of prophets nor communion of saints, no tortuous Trinity, nor endless unravelling of relationship, nature, and being. The Koran itself contains elements of Judaism, Christianity, and the pagan religions of Arabia; its vocabulary reveals Greek, Aramaic, even Abyssinian influences. But the message is plain: *He is God, the One and Only. God, the Eternal, Absolute. He begetteth not, nor is He begotten. And there is none like unto Him.* That is the burning conviction of Islam, for which Jewish ideas, Greek words, Latin inscriptions, and Byzantine columns are only the fuel. The form of the Great Mosque is the cry of the *muezzin* in stone.

The Mosque of Sidi Oqba is a world. At the gate there is always a blind beggar, a little knot of solemn children. Pale, undernourished students in groups of two and three talk quietly between Koranic classes. In the calm clearing of the courtyard men meet, kiss their forefinger in greeting, and stroll under the colonnades in earnest conversation. Officials of the Mosque, in neatly pleated turbans and short clipped beards, walk unhurriedly across the pavement and disappear through private doors. An old man dozes on a warm stone in the sun. There are no women, or very few—they prefer the Mosque of Sidi Sahib or a neighbourhood shrine. This is a man's world. In the centre of the courtyard a sundial tells the time of prayers and fasting. Beneath the pavement cisterns collect the rain water, and sockets of ancient columns, hollowed out, serve as well mouths, their lips deeply grooved by the ropes. A man lowers a bucket and prepares to wash himself before prayers. *When you rise up for prayer, wash your faces, and your hands up to the elbows, and lightly rub your heads and your feet up to the ankles.* Every aspect of life, from the most spiritual to the most carnal, is regulated. *Establish worship, pay the poor-due, and bow your heads with those that bow. . . . Forbidden unto you are carrion and blood and swine-flesh . . . and the strangled, and the dead through beating. . . . Tell the believing women to lower their gaze and be modest, and to display of their adornment only that which is apparent, and to draw their veils over their bosoms. . . . For divorced women make provision in kindness: a duty for those who ward off evil.* What the Koran does not enjoin, *hadith* or tradition takes care of. You will use your right hand for eating, your left for unclean things. You will not spit or relieve yourself in the direction of Mecca. You will not carry the Koran lower than your waist nor place another book upon it. Islam is ringed round with taboos, areas of life where no question is permitted lest society perish. The Athenians tried to do without them and lost their cohesion. The French since Descartes and the Marquis de Sade have embarked on the stimulating but dangerous experiment. Many of the taboos of Islam seem trivial, parochial, outdated, and harsh. But Islam survives.

In the dim cavern of the prayer-room, a group of students sits on amber mats in a broken circle about their teacher. They are committing verses of the Koran to memory. Everything they need to know is there, for it is a transcription of a book inscribed on tablets in heaven. They buzz over the pages like bees extracting nectar from a garden to store in the hive. In front of the *mihrab*, a man prostrates himself in prayer. *God is as close as the vein in a man's neck.* From the top of the minaret, the voice of the *muezzin* rings out over the courtyard, over the rooftops and across the *bled*. *God is most great. I testify that there is no god but God. I testify that Muhammad is the Messenger of*

God. Come to prayer. Come to salvation. God is great. There is no god but God.

The time has come to tell of the fate of Jamila, although it had nothing to do with Kairwan. I had not seen her since my marriage and had heard no news of her for more than a year. Political tension had accomplished what the *imams* and *shaikhs* never could: the nights of Ramadan were suspended for several years—by the Moslems as a sign of mourning, by the French authorities as a measure of security. Dancers and musicians were not permitted to perform in public, and I no longer went to weddings with Laila. Then one day I read a short and shocking paragraph in the local newspaper. I knew an Arab at police headquarters in Tunis and went to see him for confirmation and details. This is what he told me.

A merchant from a small town in the *bled* came to Tunis on business. It was his first visit to the capital in many years, and he brought with him a young man of the village to relieve him of the chores and tedium of the journey and to help him cope with the big city. They took rooms in a modest hotel in the Medina. Like business trips the world over, this one combined a bit of pleasure. One evening the merchant's young companion went out to procure a woman for each of them and to bring them back to the hotel. One of the women was Jamila. As taste—or fate—would have it, the young man kept the other girl for himself and sent Jamila to the merchant's room.

Early next morning the two men left the city. In the old man's room Jamila's body was found, stabbed in the heart.

"Did they find the merchant?" I asked my friend in the police.

"Of course. The hotels report the names of all visitors to the police. It was her uncle."

I was stunned. So Jamila's fears of her family had been justified.

"You see," the policeman went on, "she came of a very respectable family in the south. But her mother had been divorced and brought the child here with her to Tunis. I think the mother was not a very good woman. Then she died, and the girl had to make a living."

"What will happen to the uncle?" I asked.

"Nothing. He had to avenge the disgrace. Of course, some arrangements must be made."

I tried to picture the encounter in the hotel room. Apparently there had been no struggle, as the merchant left the next morning without arousing suspicion. "Did he recognise her immediately?" I asked.

"That was the bad part—the worst." The policeman's eyes were dark pools of condemnation, but not for the murderer. "He *had* to kill her, then."

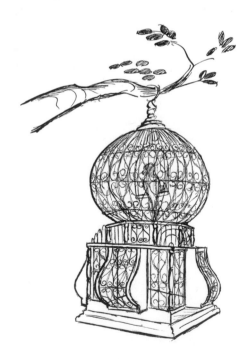

X. THE SOUTH

HERODOTUS, IN HIS SURVEY OF THE AFRICAN COAST, MENTIONS the tradition that the goddess Athene was ·born in Libya. "There is a belief among these people," he writes of the tribes that lived on the shore of lake Tritonis, "that Athene is the daughter of Poseidon and the lake, and that having some quarrel with her father she put herself at the disposal of Zeus, who made her his own daughter." After reporting this piece of divine intelligence, he goes on prosaically to the evidence. "It is evident, I think, that the Greeks took the *aegis* with which they adorn the statues of Athene from the dress of the Libyan women; for except that the latter is of leather and has fringes of leather thongs instead of snakes, there is no other point of difference. Moreover, the word *aegis* itself shows that the dress represented in the statues of Athene is derived from Libya; for Libyan women wear goatskins with the hair stripped off, dyed red and fringed at the edges, and it was from these skins that we took our word *aegis*. I think that the crying of women at religious ceremonies also originated in Libya— for the Libyan women are much addicted to this practice, and they do it very beautifully." Herodotus also tells the story of how Jason aboard the *Argo* was blown off his course and fetched up in the shoal waters off the lagoon of Tritonis. Triton himself appeared (some say it was Athene in her goat-skin) and showed Jason the way clear, in exchange for a bronze tripod the Argonauts were taking as an offering to Delphi.

The lake of Tritonis is the present salt marsh of Shott al-Jarid, and the shoal waters in which Jason was trapped were the Gulf of Gabès, the Little Cyrte of antiquity. The farther south in Tunisia the farther back in time one goes, till history fades into legend and legend into mythology. The islands of Kerkenna near Sfax are thought to have been the home, and may still bear the name, of a woman who turned men into swine. The Gulf of Gabès has been identified by certain mythogeographers as Atlantis, and geologists tell us that it is in fact a recent conquest by the sea of a land of which only the islands of Kerkenna and Jerba survive. The shore is still unsettled, full of shoals and shallows, and—a rare phenomenon in the Mediterranean—runs an eight foot tide.

Approached from the north, the country round Gabès looks like the beginning of the desert. The landscape is inhospitable, more rugged and rocky than the *bled*, with bare brooding hills and empty, monotonous plains. In summer the sun bakes the naked earth like bricks in a kiln; in winter sharp winds lift the sand and carry it across the plain. The *sebkhas* stretch for miles, their shores mottled with tufts of grey drinn. But to a traveller from the south, Gabès offers the first faint promise of a greener land. The desert is abruptly relieved with the refreshment of oases nourished by underground springs; the lean and the fat alternate here not in time, but in space. Gabès is an oasis on the shore. Gafsa is a mountain oasis. Jerba is an oasis in the sea.

Gabès is as refreshing as a bath after the long, dusty drive from Sfax. From the heat-struck glare of the road, you enter, almost without transition, into a cool orderly jungle under a roof of date palms. A broad stream flows slowly from the inland springs into the gulf; canals run in silver coils beside the road, and you drive several feet above the gardens between tabias of young palms. In the checkered shade ripen apricots, pomegranates, henna, tobacco, bananas, and alfalfa so rank it is cut ten times a year. At the ford of the stream, bare-faced women squat washing clothes, and bare-assed little boys splash in the shallows. The people of Gabès are of mixed blood. According to Pliny, one fourth of the population was Canaanite. Roman Tacapae which stood here was the northern limit of Tripolitania and the terminus and wholesale market of the Saharan slave trade. Today one of the villages is inhabited entirely by Jews; another is built into caves along the river bank. Pieces of ancient Tacapae are incorporated in the mud houses. One market place has a grandiose portico of its columns, and the mosque of Sidi Baba, patron of the oasis, is built entirely of old stones.

Unfortunately, Gabès has a heart of dust. The blessings of civilisation have bequeathed it a centre of gridiron streets, stony-faced public buildings, a cinema, several filling stations, and a discouraged park. Today the town has a new lease of life as a terminus for Saharan oil. During the Protectorate it had the seedy exoticism of a Graham Greene novel—boredom, dust, and the end of the line. Outside the Restaurant Franco-Musulman the carpet sellers buzzed and stuck like flies, and followed you inside to be shooed off by waiters flapping napkins. A group of tough-looking NCO's from the local camp drank Pernod glumly in a corner. From pigeon-holes marked with their names, the civilian railway employees picked up their spinach-streaked napkins.

But even Gabès has had its excitements. Bullet holes pock the stone faces of the public buildings and there are several gaps in the gridiron. For the oasis had the misfortune to be situated only a few miles from the Mareth Line, a southern version of the Maginot strategy, built in 1939 to stop a possible Axis invasion from Italian Tripoli. As it happened, things worked out the other way round. With Vichy acquiescence, the Germans occupied Tunisia unopposed, and the Mareth Line protected *them* from the British. It took almost a month of heavy fighting for the British to break through. German and

British tanks lie rusting in the desert, and the dead of both armies are buried in military cemeteries in the vicinity. It is sobering to come on these memorials of foreign wars in such improbable places. They make one wonder how it would feel to have one's home turned into a battlefield by other people.

There is a story told of the last war, about a Frenchman who came out here to live after the collapse of France. He had a property in the south and retired to it with his young son, a boy of ten or twelve, to wait for things to settle. The land was far from rich, but there was a house on it and the farm produced enough for the two of them. They stayed there quietly, undisturbed even by the German occupation.

But the property was in the path of the British invasion and the area was in dispute for several weeks. One day a German patrol occupied the farm house, forcing the owner and his son to move to an outbuilding. While they were there a lone British soldier, evidently lost, wandered on to the farm and was shot by the Germans. The body was left where it fell and during the night the patrol withdrew from the farm.

The Frenchman discovered the corpse the next morning. With the help of his son he carried it behind the outbuildings and left it there while he pondered what course to take. During the night he decided the safest course was to bury the body as quickly as possible and say nothing to anyone. But the next day he found that the bedouin had got there first and had stripped the corpse of clothing and equipment and every piece of identification. The Frenchman and his son dug a grave and buried the naked corpse.

Soon the British advance overran the Frenchman's property. Within two days a British officer appeared at the farm. He told the Frenchman that they had received a report of the shooting of a British soldier. The farmer at first denied all knowledge, but the officer even knew about the burial and the location of the grave. The Frenchman thereupon related

Jerba—a farm

the whole story. The officer questioned the Frenchman's son, who corroborated his father's account. The Englishman left, still undecided.

The fighting continued; the line shifted; and the Germans regained control of the area. A German officer accompanied by two enlisted men arrived at the farm. Information had been received, the officer stated, that a German soldier had been shot and buried on the farm. The Frenchman told him that the dead soldier was British and denied that he had shot him. He took the Germans to the grave, and the officer ordered his men to exhume the body. They dug up the corpse but found no identification. As it was beginning to deteriorate, the officer ordered it to be covered with earth again. He questioned the son but appeared not to believe him. Threatening the farmer with further investigation, the German left.

The British Eighth Army pushed the Germans northward and went on to liberate the east coast town by town. A French military force moved in behind them and took over the government of the region. The officer in charge was a tough Gaullist with a strong contempt for all who had stopped the fight when France surrendered. He sent for the Frenchman to come to his headquarters. There he informed him that the Liberation Army had proof that the farmer was a collaborator and had murdered an Allied soldier and hidden the body on his farm. The Frenchman went through the same weary story; he appealed to his son for confirmation but the boy had become slightly unhinged by the affair and was a poor witness. The corpse was again exhumed and, now past recognition, it was taken away. Feeling ran high in post-War Tunisia between the 'liberation' French and the 'defeatists', and the farmer was put in prison. After many delays and long investigation he was ordered to return to France and his property was confiscated.

The farm was never a good one, and the damages of war and subsequent neglect made it an uninteresting proposition. When

I saw it, six or seven years afterwards, it was derelict. Bedouin were living among the abandoned buildings.

Both the British Eighth Army and Herodotus' exploring Greeks entered Tunisia from the south. This was also the route of Sidi Oqba, and the Hilalian blight spread in the same direction. The southern gateway is a corridor pressed between the sea and the mountains. The coastline at this point turns from the vertical to run more or less horizontally across the top of Libya. The mountains of Ksour turn the same corner a few miles inland. The littoral, or corridor between, is known as the plain of Arad.

A corridor is a dangerous place to live, and Arad has an air of having been trampled by many feet in a hurry to go elsewhere. The floor is broken by a ravaged *wedd*, an outcropping of mammiform hillocks, and great boulders that might have been thrown down from the sky. The light is harsh and unfiltered by day, and dusk falls with melancholy suddenness. I have been overtaken by nightfall on Arad; even in a car, with companions, one feels an elemental loneliness and longs for the sight of human habitation.

Yet there are people who live in Arad. On some of the fallen boulders, tiny villages perch like cats that have scrambled to safety. In the middle of the plain is a town that would have pleased the White Father on my ship: Medennine is a monument to fear. The old town is a collection of apartment houses, composed of *ghorfas*—tubular cells of rubble and clay, shaped like slightly pointed Quonsett huts. The cells are laid in rows, their sides touching, and the rows are piled on top of each other to a height of four or five storeys. Each cell is separate, without communication to the others. The upper ones are reached by ladder-stairs of poles or stones stuck in the walls, and each cell has a small door through which a man can hardly squeeze. There are no windows. One can imagine the inhabitants, each family withdrawn into its cell, huddling in the airless dark till the current conqueror had passed by. Somehow, the *ghorfas* look more primitive than even tents or huts of straw; the regular form and irregular workmanship seems to spring from a collective instinct, like that of ants or bees, rather than from human intelligence. Medennine is a hive, not a town.

But the rock-nester and hive-dwellers of Arad were the brave ones. Most of the natives of the south fled to the hills. There they went literally underground. Matmata, the northern spur of Jebel Ksour, is a country of troglodytes. Tunis and other cities are filled with men from Matmata who have left their families to seek work. It is easy to see why. There is no living to be made in the hills of Ksour. The lower slopes are gravelly; above them tower cliffs and pinacles of naked rock. The villages are as inconspicuous and inaccessible as they can be. Some are built on the highest escarpments and fashioned of the same stone. Others cling to the cliff face; their streets are ledges, and their insides hollowed out of the mountain. Nearby a few terraces support a narrow strip of grain, and a couple of scrub olives grip the valley wall. The country of Matmata is not worth an invader's attention.

The true troglodytes live on—or rather in—the plateaux of Matmata and Hadege. Driving up the slopes we saw a man disappear into the hillside, closing a door behind him—for all the world like an Arthur Rackham drawing for a story about gnomes. Atop the plateau were a mosque and some grave-stones, and at a distance a police post. The rest was a field of small craters. We walked to the edge of one and looked down: the crater was the courtyard of a house, and we were standing on the roof. It was roughly square with doors on all sides; a ladder leaning against one wall led to another opening on the upper floor which was right beneath our feet. A donkey quietly munched a heap of hay twenty feet below us. As we watched, a woman in bedouin dress came out of one of the doors, looked up at us without interest as if used to having sightseers on her roof, and disappeared into a tunnel which led to one of those Rackham-esque doors in the side of the plateau. Later a guide from the police post took us through one of the houses. The rooms were hollowed out of sides of the crater and furnished with blocks, ledges, and niches carved of the same soft earth. They are well insulated from weather, but dark and infested with fleas. More than one family live in some craters, and then it is a village square rather than a courtyard. There are neither real wells nor springs in the area, but the troglodytes have dug cisterns on the same principle as their homes.

But these holes were not the original homes of the troglodytes. "Old" Matmata stands on two rocky peaks a short distance away. The houses here are partly excavated, but also partly erected above ground. Even in ruin they look more like human habitations. The subterranean somehow implies the subhuman, a kingdom of moles, snakes, and small animals with no protection but concealment. The people of Matmata reverted from a somewhat higher state to a more primitive one. What fear, I wondered, had driven their ancestors underground? In order to answer such a question, one must know just who the natives of North Africa are.

Herodotus gives the names of more than a score of tribes living between the Nile and the Pillars of Hercules in the 5th century B.C., and with a journalist's eye for curious detail he records the differences between them. The Adrymachidae for example "when they catch a bug on their person . . . give it bite for bite before throwing it away." Among the Nasamones "each of them has a number of wives, which they use in common . . . when a man wants to lie with a woman, he puts up a pole to indicate his intention." On the other hand, the women of the Gindanes "wear leather bands around their ankles, which are supposed to indicate the number of their lovers . . . so that whoever has the greatest number enjoys the greatest reputation for success in love." The Garamantes "avoid all intercourse with men, possess no weapons of war, and do not know how to defend themselves . . . The Machlyes let the hair grow on the back of their head, the Auses on the front. . . . The Atarantes, the only people in the world, so far as our knowledge goes, to do without names . . . curse the sun when it rises and call it all sorts of opprobrious names, because it wastes and burns both themselves and their land." Then there are the Atlantes, who live near Mount Atlas, "eat no living creature, and never dream." And the Gyzantes "whose country is very well supplied with honey—much of it made by bees, but even more by some process which the people have discovered. Everybody here paints himself red and eats monkeys."

But Herodotus adds: "One other thing I can add about this country: so far as one knows, it is inhabited by four races, and four only, of which two are indigenous and two not. The indigenous people are the Libyans and Ethiopians, the former occupying the northerly, the latter the more southerly parts; the immigrants are the Phoenicians and the Greeks." The Ethiopians were, of course, the black-skinned people from south of the Sahara. The Libyans were the people of North Africa. In Roman times they were called Numidians, Gaetulians, or Mauretanians, depending on where they lived. Today we call them Berbers. Modern anthropologists agree with Herodotus: the Libyans, or Berbers, whether they live in the Egyptian desert or on the Atlantic coast, are members of a single ethnic group that has preserved its racial characteristics throughout history. Egyptian wall paintings fourteen centuries before Christ depicted Libyan warriors with white skins, fair beards, and blue eyes. The blond Berbers who impress travellers today as they did the Egyptians are an original type and not descendants of lost centurions or crusaders. The majority have brown hair and eyes and their skin is darkened by the sun. They in no way resemble Arabs: they look like Euro-peans, something Celtic or Swiss, not Nordic or Latin.

Many 'Arabs' and 'Jews' of Tunisia today are detribalised Berbers. But there are also villages and whole regions that are essentially Berber in race and traditions. In parts of Algeria and Morocco the Berber strain is very pure, and the Arabs and Berbers are conscious of being two different people. In Tunisia the distinction is blurred by other differences, that be-tween Moslems and Jews, or between nomads, peasants, and townsmen; and by the influx of even newer races. But Berber ways persist. The language, a Hamitic dialect related to Coptic and ancient Egyptian, is still spoken in remote places, though there is probably no one left in Tunisia who speaks only Berber. Some Berbers have been nomadic for centuries; others settled in the same place for at least 3000 years; a few tribes have migrated and colonised new areas within recent memory. The tribes are grouped into great, loose confederations. Society and political activity are strikingly democratic, and even women have a say in tribal affairs.

The name 'Berber' is sometimes traced to the Greek for barbarian; Arab historians relate it to an imitation of stammer-ing, a slur on Berber speech; the Berbers themselves claim descent from an eponymous ancestor. The modern equivalent for the Greek and Arab attitudes is the French contention that the Berbers are a people without history. I have never under-stood what this phrase means. Presumably every race has existed as long as every other and a lot must have happened to it in that time. Does it mean that the non-historic people have usually lost their wars and failed to impose their own ways on their neighbours? Or does it merely mean that their exploits have not been recorded and we are therefore ignorant of them? A history of the Berbers could be written. It would take a man like Herodotus to do it, curious, tolerant, sceptical, and im-partial. It would require an imaginative study of the Berbers' own traditions and the reports of those who have observed them through the ages. And it would involve taking certain episodes in the history of others and turning them inside out, looking at them not from a Punic, Roman, or Arab point of view, but from that of the native North African.

A history of the Berbers might begin at Gafsa, the mountain oasis and citadel seventy miles west of the Gulf of Gabès. Capsa, to give it its old name, was an important centre in Punic times, and in view of its copious springs and position on a natural caravan route, one might guess that its importance descended from prehistoric times. In fact, traces of a late Palæolithic culture have been found there, the highest known for the period. Some skulls discovered in a cave nearby reveal that Capsian man was Cro-Magnon, the first of our species that would not arouse comment outside a zoo today. Capsian culture is believed to have spread into the Sahara and along the Algerian coast, and Cro-Magnon groups may have crossed the land-bridge then connecting Cap Bon and Sicily to colonise Europe. Not a bad beginning for a people without history.

When the Greeks and Phoenicians arrived in Africa, they found the homogeneous, sparsely scattered, pastoral people—worshipping Athene, making honey, painting themselves red—that Herodotus described. With the founding of Utica and Carthage, these people became the customers and suppliers of the new emporia. Berber troops were engaged as mercenaries in the Punic armies. Some natives were no doubt drawn into the populace of the city states, as labourers, servants, perhaps even nurses and wives. Berber words for local practices and products must have entered city speech, as Punic words and ideas were carried inland on the currents of trade and war. Inscriptions at Dougga in both Punic and Libyan show a meeting of minds and mingling of peoples. But beyond the pale of the Phoenician city states, the Berbers prosecuted their own wars, alliances, migrations, and dynasties, unaware no doubt that they were also beyond the pale of history.

Some of their activities had historic consequences. Both Carthage and Rome had African allies in the Punic Wars. Two Berber kings, Massinissa and Syphax, stepped briefly into the full light of history during the second Punic War, and the third was a direct consequence of a quarrel between Carthage and a Berber ally of Rome. After the destruction of Carthage, North Africa resounded with the clash of arms and the rise and fall of kingdoms, no matter how muffled the tumult was to European ears. Rome's decision to adopt direct rule of her empire was forced on her by the struggle between two Berber kings, Juba and Jugurtha, and was a step that hastened the end of the Republic. At the Battle of Thapsus, a few miles from Sousse, Berbers again fought for both Pompey and Julius Caesar.

Were the Berbers simply the Irishmen of their day, enjoying a good fight, no matter whose? The soldiers fought for pay: the chiefs and kinglets expected their reward in support against rivals and extension of their own authority. But I think there was more than wages and rivalry at work. The Berbers seem to enter history whenever one foreign master is in decline and another not yet established. The destruction of Carthage by Rome was one such juncture, the Arab invasion another. The latter moment especially was a node of possibilities. Certain Berbers joined a rebel Byzantine governor in founding an independent state at Sufeitula, but were defeated by the first Arab invaders. Others welcomed the Arabs and fought with them against the Byzantines. Later they turned against the invader and helped defend Byzantine Carthage. The great leader Kusaila combined the factions and achieved for a time independent control of the interior. Finally, a Berber Joan of Arc appeared and inspired the tribes to fierce resistance of Islam and its conquests. Known to history only as al-Kahena, 'the priestess', this remarkable woman seems to be a figure of legend intruding into historical times. Al-Kahena is said to have fortified the amphitheatre at El Jem and to have inflicted at least one serious defeat on the Arabs at Bagai. But, by clever diplomacy, the invaders broke up the alliance she had forged and with the help of other Berber chiefs defeated the Kahena at Gafsa in 703. After that the Kahena returns to the legend from which she emerged: some say she fell on her sword at the moment of defeat, others that she retired to the mountains and resisted the Arabs for many more years. The mighty effort ended in defeat, but for a moment the Berbers grasped the hem of freedom.

Then they merge into the stream of Arab history. Without their numbers and enthusiasm the conquest of the Maghreb, Spain, and Sicily might never have taken place. Berber dynasties came to power in Morocco and Spain. In Kairwan they first brought the Mahdi to power, then ruled for the Fatimite Caliphs in North Africa. Bad luck and bad management again defeated them, but historical reality is surely not a question of failure or success. Today, in independent Tunisia, it is not entirely fanciful to suggest that the Berber strain has come into its own.

Very well, you say (you Greeks, Arabs, and French historians), but what have the Berbers contributed to civilisation? What have they even preserved of their own creation?

The birth of Athene was no small contribution to world culture. Saturn and Caelestis also show African traits. Pagan religions were not exclusive. We know from certain inscriptions that the representatives of imperial Rome joined in the honours paid to genii of local jurisdiction. When the spiritual perspective of the world shifted to monotheism, the Berbers also adopted the worship of more jealous gods. Some tribes embraced Judaism, which they still profess. Christianity, though a phenomenon of cities, made native converts. When the apostles of Islam arrived we have seen how the Berbers, despite snubs and rebuffs, flocked to the standard of the Prophet.

There is of course nothing shameful about borrowing one's religion. We of the West are the most sedulous of spiritual apes. The test of spiritual vigour is what one makes of the import. African Christianity was certainly the healthiest form of a faith that looked much like sickness in other places. Here no holy neurotics climbed to the tops of pillars, walled themselves in tombs, or wandered in the desert—though all these props were near at hand. Perpetua and Felicity did not betray that theatrical element in martyrdom that so disgusted the Stoics. Nor did Sts. Cyprian and Augustine wear hair shirts or otherwise mortify the flesh in the fashion that later disfigured the piety of northern Europe. African theology also was rooted in common sense, not afloat in a Byzantine ether of ratiocination. North African Christians had their eyes on heaven, but their feet were on the ground.

We usually inherit our religion, but we choose our heresy. In Roman Carthage a group of inflexible Christians repudiated their bishop for cowardly surrender of holy books to the pagan authorities. Calling themselves Donatists they insisted on the importance of personal purity and went so far as to say that the validity of the sacraments depended upon the worthiness of the priest. Their movement became the nucleus for all social unrest; escaped slaves, dispossessed peasants, fugitives and adventurers of all kinds joined them and roamed the countryside committing disorders and defying the authorities to make martyrs of them. By the beginning of the 5th century, Donatists formed the majority of Christians in the western half of North Africa. When the religion changed, the heresy remained the same. The Kharejite sect of Moslems so valued individual purity that it advocated the murder of those who strayed from the path of truth, and taught that anyone—

Marabout Nefta

"though he be a black slave"—if morally and doctrinally pure could rise to the highest office in Islam. Kharejite Berbers were at one time strong enough to seize power in both Kairwan and Tripoli. Today they are still numerous in southern Tunisia. The survival of this religious individualism suggests that the spirit of Tertullian may be native to North Africa.

But the most striking difference between North African Moslems and those of the East is the cult of the *marabouts*. Saints hardly exist in most of the Islamic world (or only on sufferance, a compromise between popular sentiment and the clear unitarianism of the Koran). In Africa, their name is legion, their presence ubiquitous, their influence all pervasive. Almost every Tunisian headland and valley, every roadside spring, every village and even the separate neighbourhoods of the large medinas hold the grave and memory of one of them. The *koubas*, or whitewashed domes, of their tombs are landmarks for sailors and travellers, comforting signs of humanity in the often bleak and inhuman landscape. One finds a bit of shade, a drink, and a rest beside them; in some, one can sleep inside. Local residents visit the shrines with friendly reverence and in pious expectation. The name of Allah may be on their lips all day, but when Tunisians want a particular favour they call on their *marabouts*, as they might approach a *caïd* through his *chaouche* or gatekeeper.

Some *marabouts* are specialists, protecting flocks or fishing boats; others specialise in certain illnesses. One who lies on a peak near Constantine is devoted to Negroes, who in turn bring meat to the eagles that guard the tomb. Sidi-bou-Saïd guarded his children from rheumatism and scorpions. Quite a few are women, addressed by the Berber title *Lalla*. There are Jewish *marabouts*, and some are revered by Moslems and Jews alike. Even the simpler Christians, Greek fishermen and peasants from Pantellaria, are said to seek their aid.

Not all *marabouts* are dead and buried. In some villages you still find men with some power of healing or prophecy, or the calm mastery of life that marks a saint, who are respected as living *marabouts*. I knew a family of them who had inherited their sanctity from a great-great-grandfather and had grown rich on the rewards of piety. One of the present incumbents drove a Mercedes Benz and kept a French mistress, rather like a minor Aga Khan.

But most *marabouts* are only a name and a shrine that have been holy as long as anyone can remember. Some of their names suggest an impersonal origin—Sidi al-Mukhfi "The Hidden Lord", or Sidi Kadi al-Hadja "The Lord who Fulfils the Vows." Perhaps the spring or headland they sanctify has always been a holy spot, that Sidi this or Lalla that is merely the Arabised name of a persistent local spirit.

Herodotus wrote: "They sacrifice to the sun and moon, the worship of which is common to all Libyans, though those who live round Lake Tritonis sacrifice chiefly to Athene, and, after her, to Triton and Poseidon." In the history of ideas, monotheism is always presented as a self-evident advance over polytheism. This is one of those propositions, like the very existence of deity, that cannot be proved or disproved. We can only argue from effect, and a case can be made out from the effects of a pantheon. Religious tolerance is one: a polytheist may enslave or annihilate his enemy for many reasons, but not for idolatry. Politically, one might argue that monotheism is the image of absolutism—Pope, Caliph, and the divine right of Kings. A pantheon is a sort of parliament—exclusive, autocratic, but reversible. Psychologically, polytheism gives a man a choice of allegiance, a bargaining position with the divine, and permits him to praise or placate certain aspects of the universe without offending all others—a real danger to which the lives of holy ascetics and the discoveries of Freud attest. Finally, a multiplicity of powers may solve the vexatious problem of good and evil: there may be conflict of interest or even principle, but no catastrophe, no matter how complete, need bring the entire edifice down.

But it is late for such arguments. The world is committed to One God as it is to order, progress, efficiency, and absolute power. Strict Moslems are shocked by the cult of the *marabouts*, and would like to destroy their shrines and break their hold over the people's heart. Time after time, historic nations have tried to impose their systems on Ifriqiyah: Rome's empire was eternal; Christianity proclaimed the millennium; Muhammad was the last of the Prophets. But the white domes of the *marabouts* glow quietly on the tawny slopes and headlands like a scattered string of pearls. They are witnesses to a spirit of nonconformity that has survived on inaccessible plateaux and in hidden valleys, retreating underground when necessary, to emerge again and again, to temper orthodoxy with heresy and to challenge the pretensions of unity with the evidence of diversity. The Berber's great contribution to the world is his refusal to fit exactly the mould of progress, efficiency, and power. In despite of the imperious Idea, the Berber remains the archetype of obstinate, imperfect, enduring Man.

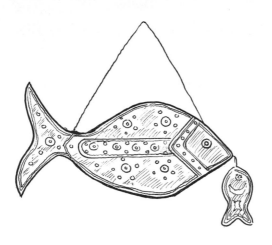

XI. JERBA

A CAMEL WENT ON BOARD AHEAD OF US. PROTESTING EVERY step on the unsteady deck, it was goaded by its lean and ragged owner to the stern, where it subsided in an uneasy crouch. On the dock a crowd of people waited to embark. They were mostly men, with faded *chechias* and unshaven jaws; but two or three women stood apart so muffled in black blankets that only their bare feet showed which way they were facing. Baskets and bundles lay on the ground beside them, and an angry chicken's head poked out from one of the black folds.

"*Ya Romi* (Hey, Christian)!" the boatman shouted and motioned us aboard. I started the engine and the car crept to the edge of the pier. Across the gunwales of the boat a few planks were laid projecting over the water several feet on each side. The crew, with weighted barrels, tilted the planks toward the dock, giving the boat a heavy list. The camel bellowed in alarm from the stern.

"It's like walking the plank," said my wife. I wondered about the chances of rolling off the other side, or whether the boat might drift away from the dock leaving us to bridge the gap. Some such expectation was in the eyes of the waiting crowd. As we inched aboard the planks sagged over the water but held fast. The boat slowly righted as we rolled athwart the gunwales, and we stopped with our front and back bumpers reflected in the water at either side. As the crew lashed us on, the disappointed audience swarmed aboard. We were off.

The island was a green and white streak on the horizon. The water rippled under us like a mottled flag, the bottom of the bay clearly visible below. Several other boats, precariously piled with passengers, livestock, and baggage, passed us, a few of them under sail. In half an hour we chugged into port. Our fellow passengers scrambled ashore and stood around waiting for us to disembark. I sympathised with them: there was no malice, but everyone enjoys a good splash. They waved good-humouredly as we drove off the quay. The camel staggered ashore last, vowing vengeance on the world.

Going to Jerba is like going to another country. It lies just off the lower lip of the Gulf of Gabès, but after the plain of Arad it could be the Antipodes. It doesn't even look Tunisian, but as if an island of the Aegean, one of the Cyclades, had come adrift and floated down to Africa. Everything is smaller than its counterpart on the mainland. We drove across the island, through groves of stunted palms, past *tabias* of coral-coloured cacti the size and shape of pink carrots. Scattered among the palms, toy houses and miniature mosques glistened like white frosted cakes decorated with little cupolas in confectionery style. Diminutive, pin-footed donkeys trotted beside the road, and the air tinkled with the bells of bicycles, the transport of small flat countries. Even the people are built to island scale. Over their all-enveloping veils, the women wear wide-brimmed straw hats tilted rakishly and giving them silhouettes like Tanagra figurines. The men in the same hats and skimpy cotton dusters have an oriental look, with fine ankles and

Jerba—the Spanish fort at Houmt Souk

Jerba—Mosque of the Turks

wrists and plump yellow faces. They are probably remnants
of an aboriginal race, for mongoloid skulls have been found
throughout North Africa. But they are Berbers now, and two-
thirds of them are puritan Kharejites. The men go out all over
the mainland and open little grocery shops; after making a
modest fortune they retire back to their island home. In the
rest of Tunisia, the name Jerbian is synonymous with grocer.

Houmt Souk—"the Market Place"—lies on the seaward
side. We arrived in mid-afternoon and found the town napping
in the feathery shade of pepper trees, the streets blank and
shuttered, the arcaded market place an abstraction of light and
shade. We went to the hotel and took a nap too.

There is nothing to *do* in Jerba—and that is a large part of its
charm. It is the traditional place for Tunisian honeymooners.
But even to the less preoccupied, the island exists in a nacreous
haze of *dolce far niente*. One may wander through the streets of
Houmt Souk and admire the architecture, also the product of
inspired confectioners. The houses wear bits of urban finery—
a spidery, useless balustrade on a roof, a fragile balcony stuck
beneath a window, a narrow door set halfway up a wall and
reached by preposterous steep stairs—that give them an air of
naïve grandeur. One of the mosques has a dome covered with
emerald scales like a lizard; another a roof of soap bubbles and
a minaret thin and pointed like a pencil. The doors are all
deliberately off centre. Many coats of whitewash make every
building look as if it had melted slightly and then hardened
again off plumb. Or one watches the inhabitants who, though
actually hardworking and industrious, seem to be staging a
quiet pageant for one's enjoyment. In the roofed souks, Moslem shoemakers fashion heel-less *babouches* of soft, creamy
leather; Jewish silversmiths make jewellery and jewel boxes in
old Turkish, even Byzantine designs; and shopkeepers sit on
stacks of blankets made in delicious pastel stripes by the island
women. In the abstract market place, jewel-coloured fish are

sold in animated auction. Down at the port coastal schooners load up with clay amphorae whose classic shape has been fashioned in Jerba probably as long as history. At night the main square, which would easily fit on the stage of any self-respecting opera house, is quickened for a few hours with masculine, coffee-drinking, pipe-smoking companionship and the hypnotic voices of half a dozen Arab radios. Around ten the electricity goes off, and the moonlight falls through the pepper trees and lies on the ground like a spotted veil.

But there *are* things to see in Jerba, if you don't sleep all day. Down at the port stands the usual Spanish-Turkish fortress, its halls silted with disuse, its fallen stones choking part of the harbour. Jerba had its share of Barbary brawls and was raped and occupied by the whole parade of Normans, Aragonese, Barbarossas, and Charles V. When the island was held by the Duke of Medina-Coeli, his entire garrison was captured and beheaded by the pirate Dragut. The Spanish skulls were then piled into a pyramidal trophy which stood near the port for four hundred years, till the European powers persuaded a 19th-century Bey to give them Christian burial. The bronze plaque that now marks the spot hardly takes their place.

Another thing to see is the synagogue of El Ghriba. The Jews of Jerba are reputedly descendants of refugees from Jerusalem, not from the destruction of the temple by Titus in A.D. 70, but from the Babylonian destruction six hundred years before Christ. Many of them are Cohens, which—being the name of an hereditary priestly class—proves their provenance from Jerusalem; and they are said to have brought a stone from the Temple with them to Jerba. Some of the men work in Houmt Souk, but they all live outside the town in two villages called Hara Kebira and Hara Sghira—which may be translated as Big Ghetto and Little Ghetto. In Little Ghetto, which incidentally is bigger than Big Ghetto, is El Ghriba, 'The

Marvellous', perhaps the oldest synagogue in continual existence in the world.

We drove inland on a rutted track that lost itself and us in a field of straggling olive trees. Both the Haras were ordinary mud-walled villages, their inhabitants indistinguishable from the Moslems of Jerba—the same diminished physiques and skimpy clothes—except that the women were unveiled and the boys had side curls under their *chechias*. At the far end of the second village were two large, pleasant, but rather characterless buildings flanking the street. One was El Ghriba. At the door we removed our shoes like Moslems and put handkerchiefs on our heads like Jews. The interior was dim and crowded. We picked our way through a log-jam of benches on which old men, wrapped in *burnouses*, sat cross-legged or lay on their backs reading the Sacred Word. Big-eyed little boys played on the floor, at home in their Father's house. It may be the oldest synagogue in the world, but it has kept up with the times and what we saw was 19th century, or later. The walls were covered with nondescript tiles, the floors with straw mats. In an inner room, a caretaker in baggy Turkish trousers unlocked a carved wooden cupboard and showed us some Torahs encased in silver cylinders. "Very old," he repeated in Arabic, and was disappointed we had no flash bulbs to take pictures. We were disappointed too, forgetting that the Jews' indifference to externals is born of their concern for what is inward.

The building across the street was a hospice for Jewish pilgrims who flock here on certain holidays. A very modern young man met us at the door; he wore a striped suit and spoke almost unbroken American. He told us he was employed by the American Joint Distribution Committee to work among the Jerba Jews. No, he was not from Jerba, but from the city—by which he meant Sousse. He was glad to show us around: ". . . a room for each family off the courtyard . . .

bring their own bedding and pots and pans . . . communal kitchens . . . ovens . . . latrines . . . another courtyard for the animals . . . empty now, but at the time of pilgrimage people come from all over the world . . . Sfax, Tripoli, as far away as Tunis." He was very brisk and efficient, and proud of his welfare work in the poor Jewish communities. I asked him if any of the Jerba Jews were going to Israel.

"All of them," he answered. "They call themselves 'Orphans of Jerusalem' and have been waiting for 2500 years to return to the Temple. But they are very impractical and must be organised. You have seen the empty houses in the villages? Why, all the bakers have left Hara Kebira, and I must arrange for them to get their bread from Hara Sghira."

I asked if he hoped to go to Israel too.

"Why should I? I have this good job, and when that is over I will join my brother in Springfield, Illinois. I am registered at the Consulate for a long time."

As we left the hospice, a lovely young woman, dressed in red and orange striped silk, with gold jewellery at her throat, sat on the doorsteps nursing an infant in her arms.

"One of the Orphans," said the efficient young man. "But she will be home soon. The last to leave here will be the Cohens. It is all planned: they will lock the door of El Ghriba for the last time. Then they will throw the key into the sky and cry, 'We have kept Thy Covenant, O Lord!'"

But the most ancient fame of Jerba is older even than the Diaspora. Ulysses, on his return from Troy, was driven by a violent gale off his course and on to the coast of Libya. In his own words: "For nine days I was chased by those accursed winds across the fish infested sea. But on the tenth, we made the country of the Lotus-eaters, a race that live entirely on vegetable foods. We disembarked to draw water, and my crews quickly set to on their midday meal by the ships. But as soon as we had had a mouthful and a drink, I sent some of my

Jerba—the Jewish village of Hara Sgira

followers inland to find out what sort of human beings might be there, detailing two men for the duty and a third as messenger. Off they went, and it was not long before they were in touch with the Lotus-eaters. Now it never entered the heads of these natives to kill my friends; what they did was to give them some lotus to taste, and as soon as each had eaten the honeyed fruit of the plant, all thoughts of reporting to us or escaping were banished from his mind. All they now wished for was to stay where they were with the Lotus-eaters, to browse on the lotus and to forget that they had a home to return to. I had to use force to bring them back to the ships, and they wept on the way, but once on board I dragged them under the benches and left them in irons. I then commanded the rest of my loyal band to embark with all speed on their fast ships, for fear that others of them might eat the lotus and think no more of home. They came on board at once, went to the benches, sat down in their proper places, and struck the white surf with their oars."

Our indispensable guide, Herodotus, places the Lotophagi on a headland within the territory of the Gindanes, the tribe whose women wore a leather anklet for each of their lovers. The concensus of mythographers is that Jerba, which may have been a peninsula then, was the land of the Lotus-eaters.

Just what the lotus is, or was, is in dispute. Ulysses speaks of "the honeyed fruit of the plant", and Herodotus described it as "about as big as a mastic-berry, and as sweet as a date. The Lotophagi also make wine from it." Pliny identified it as *cordia myxa,* the mucilaginous fruit of a deciduous tree which, mixed with grain, was said to be the staple of certain Libyan tribes. Other writers have thought it was a kind of crab apple from which alcoholic cider was made. Modern, more ingenious researchers than I, claim to have tasted the lotus today in the fruit of a shrub that grows wild on the island. It has been identified by still others as *lagmi,* the date palm wine. But against the cider-wine theory is Ulysses' statement, borne out by other ancients, that the lotus was something to eat, not drink; and surely Ulysses was familiar with common drunkenness. And neither *cordia myxa* nor the purported wild fruit of modern Jerba is known to have hypnotic properties.

I think it was this: the Greeks had had nine days of storms at sea, and ahead lay a prospect of further wandering, hardship, and danger. The three scouts set out expecting to encounter hostility; instead the Lotophagi greeted them with unexpected kindness and gave them fruit to eat. The island, or peninsula was no doubt richer and greener than it is today—we know it supported three considerable towns in classical times. Enchanted by the friendliness of the natives and the beauty of their country, the weary sailors were ready to jump ship and settle in Jerba. Perhaps they hoped to add a thong or two to the women's ankles. The lotus fruit was incidental: after all, we have only Ulysses' word for its effect. Self-centred, insensitive, and dedicated, Ulysses was blind to enchantments (including those of Circe, the Sirens, Nausicaa, and a number of other charmers) and could only attribute his men's defection to some drugged food given them by the natives.

We decided to return to the mainland by road. This had just become possible again after a lapse of some centuries, for the old Roman causeway pointing to the south, toward the Libyan border and Tripoli, had been mended. Pirates long ago had cut it in two to provide a back entrance to the shallow harbour between Jerba and the coast, and it had lain for centuries in half-submerged blocks that could be crossed only by sure-footed camels wading behind a knowledgeable guide. We left Houmt Souk at dawn and drove through a landscape damp and glistening as if it had just surfaced from a night beneath the waves. The little houses glinted like sugar cubes under the stunted palms. Rags of mist floated across the road and the beach was tricky with real mirages and fake lagoons. There was no horizon: the island seemed suspended between sea and sky. Off the causeway, a lone fishermen crawled about in his boat busy with nets; and he too seemed hung like an animated print on an opalescent screen. The Roman road looped across the water, empty and eternal, with only ourselves to mark the 20th century. Waterfowl roosting on the edge eyed us, curious but undisturbed, as they had eyed the wading camels, the pirates, the Roman engineers, and Homeric Greeks. Jerba faded in mist behind us, and ahead lay the sharp outline of the continental coast. At El Kantara the houses and men looked enormous; the road to Tripoli stretched hard and hazardous before us. We knew just how those Greek sailors must have felt chained beneath the benches as the others sat in their proper places, and struck the white surf with their oars.

XII. THE SAHARA

TO SHOW HOW ODD FACTS CAN BE, MY FIRST TRIP TO THE SAHARA
was made as the guest of a couple who were natives of Mada-
gascar. The husband was a doctor in one of the military dis-
tricts of the south; his wife lived with their five children in the
more civilised climate of Tunis. He came home as often as he
could, and on one of his leaves they invited me to dinner (this
was before I was married). A friend told me to expect raw
eels and gnat pancakes, specialities, he said, of Malagassy
cuisine. Instead the food was excellent, French, with a touch of
Marseilles, where they had lived for many years. After dinner
we looked at albums of family photographs. This turned out
to be unexpectedly fascinating. Most were the usual grey
snapshots of relations lined up facing the cameras in slightly
outmoded clothes. Others, however, were taken at what is
apparently a Malagassy institution—family reunions which
include both the living and the dead. The latter are exhumed
every few years and given a party. The living relatives lined
up facing the camera as usual, but at intervals among them
were litters bearing the bones of the departed. It was clearly
not a sad occasion: the living faces smiled broadly, and the
skulls of deceased grandparents, aunts, and cousins looked
cheerful too.

This is a far cry from the Sahara, but here I was driving
through the *bled* to the edge of the desert with a Malagassy
lady on the way to visit her husband. She was a pretty little
brown creature, with the exquisite stillness of a Japanese, and

she did the honours of the country in clipped convent French, like a well-bred hostess. The rest of us were Americans—a vice-consul and his wife and a girl visiting them from Buffalo. It was hard to see why the latter had ever come abroad. She had a neurotic horror of dirt, and carried a large supply of D.D.T. with which she sprayed every room she slept in. As native foods didn't agree with her, she also carried a box of chocolate bars and drank only bottled water or cokes. She despised the Arabs for what she called their filthy habits. In this strange company I first saw the desert.

The Sahara invades Tunisia from the west, rising along the Algerian border to the level of Gabès and the *shotts*—or great salt lakes—that almost cut Tunisia in two. The sand dunes of the Eastern Erg break against the wall of Jebel Ksour and sweep round the *shotts* themselves to clog the valleys near Gafsa and the foothills of the high steppes. Along the bridge of sand between two of the shotts lies the Bled al-Jarid, or date palm country, toward which we now were headed. It is arid, rainless desert, but underground springs nurture a string of magnificent oases—El Oudiane, El Hamma, Tozeur, and Nefta. As we descended from the plateau of Gafsa we saw the first of them below outlined as sharply as an island at sea, an irregular dark green shape on the bleached edge of the desert.

The Malagassy doctor was waiting for us under the first grove of palms. Plump, brown, and smiling, he greeted us with rather formal friendliness and thanked us for bringing his wife. Both of them had the uninsistent desire to please of really good hosts; I wonder if all Malagassies have such civilised manners. At their instigation, the shaikh of the oasis had invited us to lunch. The shaikh's house stood, not in the shadow of the palms, for watered land is too precious to build on, but on a piece of hard, flinty ground in the blazing sun. It was a mud-walled corral covering half an acre, with living quarters for a whole clan, stockyards and storehouses for the dates, as secure and self-contained as a castle. The shaikh had only one eye, which gave him a crafty look, and greeted us with unctuous courtesy at the door. Some French Army officers were there before us. The shaikh sat down at the table, but his sons, some nearing middle age, stood and waited on us. There was an entire roast sheep with the *couscous*. The American girl ate nothing, and we told the shaikh she was ill, despite her vivacity with the French officers. Afterwards we were served black, amber, and pale saffron dates still on their branches. The shaikh spoke eloquently in praise of France and the blessings of her Protectorate, but afterwards he took the vice-consul aside and asked if he and his family could be placed under American protection.

After lunch we toured the plantation. The date comes into its own in this hot dry climate. The prickly rutted trunks rise straight as columns and burst into fine fountains of leaves and fruit at the top. Dark-skinned, wiry boys scrambled up them for branches of dates for us to take away. The sunlight filtered down as if through a *mesharabiyyah* on other trees, of olive, orange, almond, and fig, and on gardens of cereals, vegetables, and tobacco. The date palm is the olive of the desert, the staff and mainstay of life. The fruit is the cash crop; the leaves provide thatching and fences to keep out encroaching sand; the trunks make poles and beams for the houses and foot-bridges to cross the canals. With this, and their flocks for wool, meat, and milk, the oases are practically self-sufficient.

There is a snake in every Eden. Here it was the flies. Among the children who tagged along wherever we went, almost every one had an eye running and beginning to glaze with trachoma. The flies gathered round the good eyes and the bad, like animals at a water hole, their invisible footprints carrying the germ from eye to eye.

The Malagassy couple were stopping here, but they insisted on sending one of the shaikh's sons with us for our trip to the other oases. We protested, but the Shaikh ordered one of them, a large, slow, but amiable fellow named Shedley, to go with us. Shedley was about thirty; he wore European clothes and spoke passable French, but he was a very foreign addition to our now all-American party, and he took rather a lot of room. At our first stop the American girl asked me to change places with her. Shedley, she said, was pressing against her.

We had planned to spend the night at Tozeur, but the hotels were filled with the families of French officers stationed there. Though it was late, we decided to drive on to Nefta, another fifteen or twenty miles through the desert. The road was execrable, darkness began to fall, and—the usual travellers' tale—our car broke down. Shedley suddenly became very important to us. He assured us there was nothing to worry about from bandits or wild beasts, then asked if we had a gun. The vice-consul drew a revolver from the glove compartment, and Shedley nodded approval. With this assurance, he left to find help. We watched him walk to the end of the headlight beam, hesitate a moment, then plunge into the dark.

"Probably gone to signal the attack," I remarked. The vice-consul reached over and locked the doors from inside. It had grown cold with the dark, and we sat with the windows rolled up and waited.

In about an hour a dim light appeared on the road ahead and moved slowly toward us. The vice-consul switched on the headlights, but not till the light came within a few yards of us could we tell what it was: a small tractor used for road repairs, with Shedley and a sleepy driver aboard. Ignominiously, we were towed into Nefta.

The town was dark and silent as if under a curfew. The tractor hauled us through black streets and left us in front of an even blacker shape looming against the sky. Shedley banged on the door and finally persuaded a frightened porter to open up the hotel. There was no electricity: we were each given a candle and led upstairs where the porter opened a string of doors all in a row and left us. We said good night and entered our dark, close-smelling rooms. Outside, I noticed, was a latticed balcony that ran the length of the floor. I blew out my candle and went to sleep like a stone.

A scream brought me awake. I lit the candle and went out into the corridor. From a nearby room came a muffled noise of voices. At the other end of the corridor, the vice-consul and his wife appeared at their door with a lighted candle. Then Shedley's door was flung open, and out ran the American girl.

She was in her night clothes. After looking wildly from one end of the corridor to the other, she rushed toward the couple. Shedley appeared in his doorway dressed in long woollen underwear, the jacket of his suit held modestly before his middle. He looked confused and rather hurt.

I said, "*Tisbahlakhir*, Shedley," which means until the morning.

"*Tisbahlakhir*," he said and went back into the room and shut the door.

I went to the couple's room, where the girl was sitting on the bed sobbing.

"Did he touch you?" asked the vice-consul's wife.

"Yes ... he ... he *embraced* me!" sobbed the girl.

"Is that all he did?" asked the vice-consul.

"He ... he tried ... oh, it's horrible!" whimpered the girl.

"Wait a minute," I said. "*You* were in *his* room. How did that happen?"

She cried louder. The vice-consul's wife put an arm around her and the vice-consul gave her a shot of whisky from a flask. In a minute she was calm enough to tell the following story, punctuated by sniffles and sobs.

"I D.D.T.'d my room before I undressed. I looked at the bed as well as I could with only a candle, and decided to sleep *on* it, not in it. Then I undressed and lay down. I guess I fell asleep. Pretty soon, I felt *distinctly* something crawling up my leg."

"Shedley?" I asked.

"No. A *bug*! I couldn't find any matches, so I got up and sat on a chair for a while. Then I felt it *again*. I couldn't stand it! I went outside on the balcony, but it was cold. So I went along the balcony and tapped at a window."

"Shedley's?" I asked.

"I thought it was *theirs*!" She indicated the couple. "I thought that as long as you had two beds, maybe I . . . But it wasn't, it was *his*!"

"Shedley's," I said. "What did you expect him to do? Offer you a candy bar?"

She began to cry again, and the couple let her stay in their room. I went back to mine and slept undisturbed by crawling things.

The sun broke through the lattice of the balcony. Down on the square in front of the hotel the Arabs of Nefta were warming themselves in patches of light. Shedley was there too, conferring with a mechanic over the car. I got dressed and went down.

"Don't worry about last night," I said. "Just a misunderstanding."

Shedley looked puzzled and still rather hurt. "But what did the American lady want?" he asked plaintively.

"She doesn't know herself," I said. "She seems to have had an itch of some kind. Let's forget the whole episode."

Our little party was somewhat strained as we walked about the oasis of Nefta. The American girl appeared to have recovered and greeted Shedley politely, if a bit distantly. They kept the rest of us between them as we toured the oasis on foot. My chief memory of Nefta is water—a large lake, flashing streams, dams and sluice gates, canals, and waterfalls. Under one of the cascades a bunch of kids were ducking and splashing. They were naked, and one of them had just been circumcised and wore his little pecker in a sling tied with cord round his waist. But he splashed with the rest of them just the same. The American girl averted her eyes from this badge of piety and cleanliness. Here let us abandon her to her dreams of lice and licentiousness, and Shedley to his disappointed risings. They have sufficed to bring us to Nefta and the edge of the desert.

Water and religion: *marabouts*, mosques, shrines, and *zaouias* spring almost as numerous as the date palms, for Nefta is also a religious town. It is not without significance that two of the West's three great religions were conceived in the desert. The empty plains, the dry rivers, and the naked mountains remind us that there is a part of creation not designed for man. The Arabs believe it to be inhabited by *jinns*, invisible beings who are both good and bad, and to whom the Koran is addressed as much as it is to us. To the Judæo-Christian mind, it is the antithesis of the garden, of paradise, the land of milk and honey. Even to unbelievers it brings thoughts of oblivion and death. And there is worse. Bled al-Jerid lies between two *shotts* or *sebkhas*, great salt lakes that stretch more than two hundred miles from the Gulf of Gabès into Algeria. They form in a vast depression, perhaps once an inlet of the sea, which now collects the flow of wedds from the north. After the rainy season, they are shallow seas of mud; later the sun evaporates the surfaces, leaving a brittle crust over soft, viscous clay. A few tracks have been staked across them and are passable part of the year; but they lead through quicksand patches and past islands of glutinous mud, and to deviate from the track is to invite disaster. Nothing grows here. The soil is permeated with salt, which ensures sterility, like the Roman outrage intended to Carthage. It glitters like the husk of some

brazen planet or burnt-out star. Extraordinary mirages appear
—houses, cities, ships, and moving caravans. Here all the *jinns*
are bad. If the desert is negative, indifferent to human life, the
shotts are a curse—emblems of cosmic malevolence, the
triumph of the demoniac forces of the universe. They remind
us that there is something worse than death. It is hell.

But there is also grace, and this is the religion of Nefta.
Mysticism was a slow starter in Islam. Although Muhammad
himself had one of the most direct and well-documented re-
lationships with God that any man has known, there were no
mystics among his immediate followers in Arabia. It was not
till Islam spread to other nations, into Mesopotamia and Persia,
that mystical ideas began to seek outlet in the new religion. The
mystics were called *sufi* meaning "wool", at first a term of
abuse, for they were accused of wearing the white woollen
robe of the Christians. But the *sufi* sought justification in the
Koran and found it in the ecstatic passages of the Prophet.
Sufi-ism was brought to North Africa by a missionary from
Mesopotamia named Abdal Kader, and Nefta is a centre of the
cult of Kadria. (In modern times, it has gained fresh impetus
from a confusion of the founder's name with that of the
Algerian rebel Abdal Kader who defied the French and was, in
fact, a member of the Kadria sect.) In Nefta, it has become intermingled with certain pre-Islamic beliefs involving hidden,
subterranean powers. It seems plain to me that the first of these
powers must be water, for life itself depends on the deep and
bountiful springs of the oasis. Perhaps the splashing of the
docked children in the irrigation canals was the expression of
an unconscious religious rite. In a land where the sky is harsh
and inimical, one can see the importance of underground gods.

But the desert is not entirely lifeless. Animals live there—
gazelle, jerboa rats, lizards, snakes, and scorpions all eke existence. In deep underground springs, fish have been found.

After an exceptional rain, ephemeral crops of grass and flowers spring from long-dormant seeds. Leaf impressions and the petrified trunks of trees show where forests once stood; and rock drawings of elephants and giraffes tell us what the climate must once have been. Ever since the great drought set in, man has continued to live in the oases and to ply commerce across the waterless wastes. The desert is very like the ocean, with shores and ports, islands, ships and charted lanes. Sand is much the same as sea-water from man's point of view—soft, mobile, and unfavourable to life. The tides are winds; from the air you sometimes see whole oases they have conquered, with outlines of submerged buildings and the tops of drowning palms. Ancient cities have been engulfed once their dikes were down; the Arab caravaners say that their inhabitants were turned to stone by some catastrophe, and bring out marble heads and hands and the bodies of stone infants to prove it. Herodotus tells of a tribe that declared war on the south wind and marched out to the desert where the wind blew and drowned them in sand.

North Africa is in fact a large island bounded by the Mediterranean, the Atlantic, and the Sahara. Of them all, the desert has been the greatest barrier, and North Africa has always had more contacts with Europe and the Near East than with equatorial Africa. A few adventurers penetrated the Sahara early in history and some claimed to have reached the other side. Among the wonders they reported were the rain forests with their menageries of astonishing beasts and even stranger races of dwarfs and giants, a country of black Jews, and a kingdom of Negroes ruled by a white dynasty. But crossing the desert, except as a singular adventure, became feasible only after the introduction of the camel, thought to have been brought to Egypt by the Persians in the 5th century B.C. and from there taken into the Sahara by the Berbers. The ship of the desert might have been invented for its new environment.

The flat, spreading feet act like snow-shoes on the soft sand; the horny pads and tough skin cushion the crouching animal on stony ground; the proverbial abstinence and endurance take it across the long arid stretches with maximum cargo and minimum provisions. Besides this, a camel can smell water a mile away; in a long drought it can be made to vomit a potable liquid; a she-camel provides milk for drinking and dried curds for storage; the hump can be cut into for fat without killing the animal; and as a last resort the beast can be eaten.

Thanks to this remarkable machine, a steady trade began to flow between equatorial Africa and the Mediterranean world. Spices, ivory, gold, feathers, wild animals, and black slaves moved northward; salt and the products of civilisation moved to the south. Trade routes were established, and the caravans moved out from a port on the edge of the desert, stopping for fuel and rest at the island oases along the way, till they came into port on the other side.

One of these great ports on the northern shore of the Sahara is Ghadamès, near the tip of Tunisia's tail. On most maps you will find Ghadamès in the Fezzan, a province of Libya. But after the War, French forces occupied the Fezzan for several years, and the southern boundaries of Tunisia shifted like the desert sands and for a time encompassed Ghadamès. Such shifts are nothing new in the desert. Boundaries have no physical reality there, and the nomads cross them at will. In fact most boundaries in North Africa and the Near East were drawn by European powers who often ignored both geographical and political facts. To the Arabs the significant thing is not borders, but centres of power—Tunis or Tripoli, Baghdad or Damascus. Sovereignty extends as far as that power can be felt through force, attraction, or alliances. Thus the line where two such powers meet is vague and moveable. This system worked all right when the edges of power lay in useless desert and the nomads carried their loyalties with them. But the discovery of oil beneath the sand changed things: boundaries became important to Arabs too, or at least to their governments; and the two concepts are now at odds in the Arab world. Oil has been found in the Sahara now. Ghadamès is back in the Fezzan.

At the time I write of it was 'administered' by Tunisia, and Air France was trying to popularise *les Weekends à Ghadamès*. We flew, my wife and I the only takers that weekend, in a two-engined plane, crossing the desert without mishap but running into the hangar and bending a wing at our destination. Most of the European population was at the airport, like villagers to meet the weekly bus. They were all men, dressed in great black bloomers piped in white, and wide flat sandals with toes pulled up and tied in a curve like the tips of skis. This was the uniform of the Meharistes or Camel Corps, but all the Europeans affected it. We drove by jeep to the hotel—a palace of unanticipated grandeur built by the Italians in cinematic Sudanese style during the Fascist dream of empire. The hotel was still haunted by these dreams. In the lounge the old guest books provided a graph of the fortunes of war. The earliest were entirely in Italian; then German crept in; English took over a little later; and now they were written entirely in French—all with patriotic slogans and truculent taunts in keeping with the language of the moment. Our room was dark and voluptuous, with thick walls and tiny triangular windows, a Hollywoodean den of desert intrigue. At night the bar filled up with French officers in their black bloomers and clean white shirts. At dinner a Negro major domo in the same uniform chanted the menu to the entire company, and the French officers responded antiphonally with ironic, wistful memories of the dishes and wines of France.

Next day we walked round the vast plantation of date palms that shades Ghadamès like a leafy parasol. The streets run between walls of sun-dried brick; sometimes they dip under-

Camels are still being used in parts of Tunisia to draw water for irrigation.

ground to run for a stretch through dark, cool tunnels. Occasionally we passed a man, but never a woman. The men looked Caucasian with a Negro infusion, remarkably handsome and healthy, even to their eyes, and with looks of intelligence and sophistication quite different from the yokels of the Bled al-Jerid. The women, we learned, never go out; we saw some of them from a minaret, sitting on their rooftop, black draped forms condemned to eternal boredom among carpets and palm fronds. Once we saw the rule apparently broken by a heavily veiled figure bearing a water jar in the street, but at the hotel we were informed that she was certainly a slave.

The life of Ghadamès is concentrated in a wide, sun-beaten square with rows of shops and warehouses on three sides and on the fourth the city wall and a gate opening to the desert. Through the gateway the caravans arrive from the Sudan or mid-Saharan oases to discharge their freight for local consumption or trans-shipment to the north. The camels squat wearily in the dust to be unloaded. Local businessmen transact deals with the caravan leaders. Negroes wait patiently for a caravan going to some oasis that is the centre of their lives. Strollers and idlers stroll and idle with various intent. The shops display almost no goods, a little tea or sugar, a few sacks of grain, and have the faintly sinister bareness of places where only paper is exchanged.

Outside the gate an authentic Beau Geste fort faced the desert, the Tricolor flying from the ramparts, the cock-cry of a bugle crowing of order and security across the sand. French officers mingled with the crowd on the square, and Arab soldiers walked about with an engaging swagger. The latter were dark, small, and tough; they wore white tunics over their billowing black bloomers, and across each shoulder a red bandillero which formed X's front and back, giving them the look of tilted Red Cross Knights. The Meharist soldier is recruited from the Shamba, a nomadic tribe originally from

Syria that migrated to the Sahara long ago. Once there they took up the two possible professions of conducting caravans and robbing caravans. They first fought the French, then joined them. The French thereupon legalised the Shamba's natural inclinations and made them policemen of the desert.

And there were Tuareg—the pirates of the desert. They lounged about the square of Ghadamès with an air of fierce insolence—tall, angular men in tightly belted robes, turbans that looped down in a veil over their mouths and chins, and baleful, kohl-blackened eyes. Each had a dagger in his belt and carried a musket or rifle. One was dressed in violet—I had thought the Purple Tuareg were a separate tribe, but there he was—and the dye after a lifetime without baths had turned his skin the colour of dried ink. They all had fine, long hands and feet, and squatted in the dust or strode across the square with feral grace. The veil, the kohl-rimmed eyes, the wasp waists, and the languid grace made them seem a race of attenuated, slightly malevolent women.

For centuries the Tuareg ruled the Sahara. They terrorised the oases and preyed on caravans, exacting tolls and tribute, killing the rash and unwary, taking slaves, then vanishing into the depths of the desert. They were demons of cruelty and cunning. Where they lived was a mystery. The oasis-dwellers credited them with creating the sand storms which they often used to cover an attack. For years they blocked French penetration of the Sahara and gave the Empire a generation of heroic deaths. With Shamba aid and superior arms, the French finally broke their power in 1903 at the Battle of Tit. It was found that the Tuareg had never numbered more than forty or fifty thousand, with a fighting force of one quarter of that. Through mystery, courage, and the terror they inspired they had been masters of the Sahara from one end to the other.

Defeat has not dispelled the mystery. These redoubtable warriors live in a matriarchal society and claim descent from a queen called Tin Hinan. Names and inheritance descend through the female line, and the son of a Tuareg woman and a foreigner is a Targui. The veils of the men are a protection against sand, but they are never removed, even to eat and drink, and the mouth of a man is thought indecent. The women, on the other hand, go unveiled. And they are permitted, indeed encouraged, to take lovers. Queens preside at the knightly jousts and *amal*, or courts of love. In the latter, Tuareg men compete in recitations of impromptu poetry for the honours and favours of their queens. Such tokens of chivalry have led to the romantic theory that the Tuareg are remnants of a lost crusade.

The Tuareg are in fact Berbers and speak a Hamitic dialect. The nobles are thought to be pure Berber, but there are six classes shading down through priests, hereditary serfs, household slaves, and outdoor slaves; and the lower the class the blacker the skin. The nobles were converted to Islam in the eleventh century. They conquered Morocco, crossed to Gibraltar, and defeated the Spaniards in 1086. There they subjected the petty Moslem kings and ruled for a century as the dynasty of Almoravides (=*al murabit*=*marabout*). They also pushed southward, conquered the Negro empire of Ghana, and started the conversion of West Africa to Islam.

So much from books. We walked out to the Tuareg camp at Ghadamès, for they do not live in the oasis or within walls. Women were working among the tents, unveiled but unapproachable. A group of little boys crouched in a circle, with almond eyes and olive skins, their heads shaved except for a top-knot on the crown. They were friendly but shy, not yet schooled in fierceness. There were no men about—sleeping? out on the desert? or simply lounging in the square? We started back disappointed, and a little saddened as one is by the taming of a wild animal. As we dipped into a small gully, a mounted Targui loomed suddenly above us. He was dressed in black, the ashy black of dry lava, and his camel was the colour of ashes too. From below, it seemed the tallest camel I had ever seen, rising on gnarled, trunk-like legs, with sloping flanks, and spout-shaped dinosauran neck. The Targui's black skirt fell over the animal's hump, making rider and mount a single dark pyramid silhouetted against the sky. I looked up into the shadow of the veil, and as I did the Targui looked down at me. Kohl gives a peculiar shine to the eye, and perhaps his look was one of mere curiosity. But for an instant our glance clashed like blades. Then, in response to some invisible pressure of the Targui's foot, the giant camel lurched across the sky.

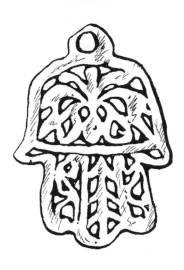

XIII. *L'ENVOI*

I MUST TELL ONE MORE STORY, OR RATHER TWO EPISODES THAT are part of a single story. It concerns Laila and my wife. The first incident is out of place here in time, as it happened not long after my marriage.

With a wife, I moved out of my bachelor quarters in Sidi-bou-Saïd and took a larger house at the foot of the cliffs, in a wild, secluded corner on the estate of the Beylical princes. It was a long climb from where Beshir lived, but Laila insisted on coming to cook for us, though we had a full-time boy to look after the house. Because of the distance, Laila was frequently late and when the weather was bad sometimes did not come at all. As a bachelor I was used to such irregularity, but with marriage my life had become much more conventional, even formal, and we decided we could not put up with it. With Laila's agreement, we hired another cook, a European woman, and Laila came in to help. Soon objects of little or no value, but

211

indispensable to us, began to disappear—and I recognized the hand of Laila trying to create suspicion of the new cook. I had this out with her, and there was a savage scene in which curses and obscenities were spattered on some female, whether the new cook or my wife I could not tell, and my temper flared. Laila then walked out. When I met her at Beshir's several days later, we embraced and were friends again, but there was no question of her returning to work for us.

Our houseboy came from another village. One day when I was at work, he came to my wife with a basket of stuffed dates which he had been given in the souks, a present from Laila. In a voice strained with fear and embarrassment, he said: "Please do not eat these dates, Madame. Throw them into the sea."

My wife was surprised, as she had heard me praise Laila's way with dates, and they looked perfectly good to her. She asked the boy why.

"Madame," he said in a solemn voice, "I am not from Sidi-bou-Saïd, but since I have been here I have heard a lot of talk in the souks. The Negress has sworn that when you leave she will return to the master and rule in his house again."

"But why should I leave?" asked my wife. "Do you mean the dates are poisoned?"

The boy looked embarrassed, but also scared. "Do you believe in witch-craft, Madame?" he asked. "I was put under a spell once by a woman who forced me to love her daughter, though I was promised to my cousin. That is why I left my last job and came to work here—to escape the spell."

"But what can Laila force me to do?" my wife asked.

"Leave the master," he said with conviction, "or—or change somehow so he will divorce you. And after all, they may be poisoned. Please, Madame, let me throw the dates into the sea."

My wife does not like sweets and would not have eaten the

dates in any case. But the boy had communicated his alarm to
her, and she told him to do what he liked with the present.

When I got home I laughed at the story and pretended to be
angry at having been done out of the stuffed dates. That
evening I went to Beshir's house, and, after kissing Laila,
thanked her for the present.

"They were for your wife," she said smiling. "I saw her in
the souks the other day: she's looking thin. Isn't she pregnant
yet?"

"She thanks you too. Will the dates make her conceive?"

"They will give her strength," said Laila. "But if you will
do what I told you to with a little fish's blood. . . ."

To this day I do not know what had been done to the
basket of dates—if anything.

How little we understand other people, especially those of
different race, customs, habits, and belief. I had thought Laila
was as familiar to me as my sisters and aunts, because she told
her beads and made a novena at the mosque, or because she
turned my clean socks inside out with the toes tucked in in
that maddening way of women the world over. I had also
thought I had seen through Jamila and dismissed her fears as
dramatic fancies. Despite intimacy and affection I had misread
them both. How can it be otherwise? We discern a few traits
that look familiar and assume that they stem from roots growing in the same soil as our own. But all our experiences, beginning with the way we are suckled, cradled, washed,
combed, and dressed, are so different that our ideas of affection,
contentment, greed, restraint—everything we are or want—
must be different too.

If other individuals are opaque to us, what insight can we
expect into a society or culture not our own? Reading the
Latin poets we think we see our emotions mirrored in theirs;
but could men who owned slaves, applauded the games, and

worshipped temporal power have the same notions of love, reverence, fear, and happiness as our comparatively spinsterish own? Allah revealed himself to a young camel-driving seer on the desert Red Sea Coast in the 7th century A.D. Does He move in an agricultural or industrial community in the same mysterious way? The nomadic bedouin with their lives of peripatetic necessity, the Jews of Jerba waiting 2500 years to return to Jerusalem, the underground but unreconstructed Berbers, the exquisitely refined Franco-Arabs of Tunis— where is the common ground on which they meet, or we meet with any of them?

After five years I felt no closer to understanding Tunisia than I had that first afternoon in Tunis when I had been repelled and repulsed by the frenetic, alien crowds. I had travelled extensively, made friends, done my homework, listened and looked with an open mind and an open heart, and become emotionally involved in the personal, social, and political life of the country. But as in Kairwan, I felt excluded from some central mystery. Despite friendship and voyages, heart and mind, there remained an enigmatic otherness. Laila's present of the dates had become a family joke with us, but it was something else as well—a riddle of birth and death, an undecipherable message of love or hate.

Ifriqiyah—the Arabs' name for Africa—has always intrigued me by its mixture of familiarity and strangeness. Originally— before it began the prodigious career that brought it to cover a whole continent—the name in both Latin and Arabic meant roughly the area of modern Tunisia north of the *shotts*. Ifriqiyah seems to me to express all the anomalies and contradictions, the richness and ambiguity of Tunisia. It contains the homeland of the Berbers and the Arab Maghreb, the Turkish Beylic and the French Protectorate, the Barbary Coast, the Roman cities, the *tell*, the desert, and the *bled*. The past is preserved in it like the stone of Carthage embedded in a gate at

Sidi-bou-Saïd or a mosque at Kairwan, or like the old patterns of living that still survive—the houses facing inward round an atrium and the family, the veils that would not have looked out of place in Pericles' Athens, the walled medieval cities, the immemorial diet of olives, wheat, and fish, the shepherd piping to his flock, the fisherman praying to a spirit that has inhabited a particular hill for all time.

But Ifriqiyah changes too and welcomes new ideas. Everyone who has come here—pirate, crusader, pilgrim, administrator—seems to have contributed or altered something, a new name for an old object, a useful plant or agreeable flower, the shape of a tool, a form of contract, or a way of acknowledging God—a small pebble or broad pattern in the mosaic, some slight or profound difference in the way things might otherwise have been. Both Christianity and Islam took root and produced notable crops in her soil. Under the Protectorate, Tunisians flocked to French schools and to France itself to study; the intellectual freedom and liveliness of French civilisation appealed to the most civilised country in Barbary, and that, not politics or plumbing, is the precious legacy of France in Ifriqiyah. From the rich humus of the past, Ifriqiyah continued to produce new and original presents and futures. Today, as the Republic of Tunisia, she manages the unaccustomed role of independence and democracy as if to the manner born. Tomorrow, she looks forward to further transmutations based on Saharan oil and a federation of North African states.

Ifriqiyah is not just a transplantation, nor the product of crossing many foreign stocks. The name itself has a native root. Some think it comes from a Berber word meaning coolness used by the tribes of the interior to describe the ocean-blown peninsula of Cap Bon. Others say that the first Phoenician scouts landing near the site of what was to be Carthage or Utica found natives living there who called themselves

'Afri'. (It is part of the irony and paradox of the word that it should now signify a continent that contains some of the hottest countries in the world and races as dissimilar as they can be to the Berbers of Utica or Cap Bon.) But the obscurity of its origin may be taken as symbolic too: of the elusive native quality, the nameless correspondence behind the erosions of the Arab tongue, the smiling sensuality of Sousse, the pious laughter of Sidi Amor's tomb in Kairwan, the sorrow of an Andalusian song, the enormities of Karakouz, the business acumen of Sfax, the political flair of the young Republic. It is there, quietly turning all the borrowings and impositions into the substance of Ifriqiyah. All her lovers and despoilers have come up against it, this irreducible otherness. It is Tunisia's final, irremovable veil.

Respect for this otherness is what a love of Ifriqiyah teaches. Terence, who was born a slave at Carthage, wrote: "I am a man, and nothing that is human is alien to me." In the hospitable climate of Barbary, the differences between men have grown and flourished; and the differences, after all, are more interesting than the similarities. A spirit of easy, if imperfect, tolerance has permitted individuals and communities to live side by side for generations and centuries, keeping their separate customs, creeds, and idiosyncracies. And this, it seems to me, is the healthiest kind of society, one that respects the differences among its components and from their diversity draws its strength.

The time came when we had to leave Tunisia for good. We were sad, leaving the only home we had known together, our mutual friends and most of our mutual memories. Even in five years one puts down roots that ache somewhat at being pulled up. But we were also excited, and a little relieved. I was beginning to find my compatriots rather peculiar and home a strange sounding place. My wife had never lived in America, and I was eager to show it to her. Besides, we were expecting our first child in about two months. We were ready to begin a new life.

In a muddle of expectancy and regret we packed our things, closed our house, and said goodbye to our friends. Laila was not at Beshir's house when we went to call; she had taken a job in a hospital nearby and came home late at night. On the day our plane was to leave my wife and I went back to our denuded house to take a last sentimental look at Sidi-bou-Saïd and the view across the bay. We were standing on the terrace when suddenly Laila appeared. It was the first time she had come to us since the day she had stalked out in a fury.

She was completely veiled in a white *ha'ik* and little black mask, and for a moment she stood silently before us, one dark hand against her breast, breathless from her walk down the hill. Then she pulled off the mask and revealed a radiant smile. She reached into her bosom and brought out another present— a silver Hand of Fatma. She slipped the chain over my wife's head and kissed her on the mouth.

"Beshir's father gave it to me." she said, "when I was married. It will keep you from harm. May Allah bless you with a boy."

I offered to drive her back up the hill but she refused. She kissed me and then pulled the *ha'ik* over her head and face. "God keep you in peace," she said huskily, her plum-coloured eyes damp above the veil. By this time, my wife and I were in tears too. The last we saw of Laila was her thick white form trudging up the cliff road.

The international airport of Alouina lies halfway between Tunis and Sidi-bou-Saïd on the lake shore. As the plane circled after take-off, we saw tilted beneath us the familiar landscape of the past five years, already remote and formalised by distance as it soon would be by time. The marshy edge of the lake, with its skein of roads and the bent track of the sea-going railway, were suddenly clear and logical, like cartographers' symbols. Automobiles, some no doubt containing the friends and colleagues who had just seen us off, moved mechanically on errands no longer any concern of ours. The plane plied across a saucer-shaped world, like the self-contained cosmographies of the ancients. At the bottom of the saucer, the lake lay serene and unruffled by our passage. Bou Kornine and the Mountain of Lead assumed the ideal forms and jewel colours of themselves in a painting by Beshir. Tunis was barely legible in the distance. The line of shabby, historical suburbs—La Marsa, Carthage, La Goulette—lay on the rim of the saucer between the lake and the bay. As we left the land we saw Sidi-bou-Saïd, white and perfect like something cast up from the deep, a shell one picks up and takes home, the indestructible essence of a summer by the sea. Then we were over the water—a deep, miraculous blue, containing all the colours of infinity.

CHRONOLOGY OF TUNISIAN HISTORY

Pre-History   In late Palæolithic times Cro-Magnon men
developed a high level of culture near Gafsa in
central Tunisia, may have colonised Europe via
Sicily. In Neolithic times North Africa was invaded by races of unknown but varied origin.
As history dawns, the people now known as the
Berbers inhabited all Africa north of the Sahara,
having different customs but striking racial and

B.C.   linguistic unity, as noted by Herodotus in the
5th century.

11th century   Phoenician traders founded the emporium of
Utica near modern Bizerta. 850 is the traditional

9th century   date of the founding of Carthage by Phoenicians
from Tyre led by a princess, Elissa or Dido.
Carthage soon became the leading city of the
west, conquering Spain and sending expeditions
into the Atlantic as far as Britain and Senegal.

264–241   Carthage collided in Sicily with expansionist
Rome in the First Punic War. Hamilcar Barca
was one of the defeated Punic generals, but lived

218–201   to reconquer Spain. His son Hannibal crossed by
land from Spain into Italy, where he fought the
Second Punic War for fifteen years. Scipio
carried the war to Africa and defeated Hannibal
at the Battle of Zama. Carthage was shorn of her

149–146   possessions. The Third Punic War was a Roman

seige of Carthage that lasted three years, ending in the capture and complete destruction of the Punic city.

44 Julius Caesar refounded Carthage with his veterans. Roman Carthage rapidly became the capital of Africa again. In 180 the first Carthaginian Christians were martyred. Tertullian,

A.D. St. Cyprian, and St. Augustine were members of the African church which so stamped the character of western Christianity.

435 The Vandals conquered Carthage, making it the base for a pirate kingdom that controlled all North Africa. A century later Belisarius led an

534 expedition against the Vandals and 'restored' Carthage to the Byzantine Empire.

648 The first Arabs raided southern Tunisia. The
670 city of Kairwan was founded by Sidi Oqba as the base for the Moslem conquest of the west. The

9th century golden age of North African Islam came under the Aghlabite dynasty in Kairwan. Tunisian Arabs invaded Sicily in 827 and remained there till driven out by the Normans in the 11th

909 century. The Fatimites seized Kairwan and from there conquered Egypt and Syria, founding Cairo in 972. They left a Berber vassal (the Zirides) to rule for them in Africa, but these became disloyal and were punished by an onslaught

1051 of Egyptian nomads, known as the Hilalian invasion, which destroyed the economy and future fertility of Tunisia. Simultaneously, Normans, Pisans, and other European adventurers occupied the coastal towns. A Moroccan dynasty, the

1230 Hafsites, pacified and united the country and established their capital at Tunis.

15th century   Arabs and Jews, expelled from Spain, resettled in North Africa.

1534   A Turkish corsair, Kheireddine Barbarossa, seized power in Algeria and Tunisia, deposed the last Arab king of Tunis. Charles V disputed the conquest, and fighting between Turks and

1574   Spaniards raged for forty years. The Turks won, and piracy became the essential industry of the

1707   state. A Cretan captain of cavalry, Hussein Ali, seized power in Tunis and founded the dynasty of Beys that lasted till 1957.

1830's   France occupied Algeria, began interfering in Tunisia. Deprived of piratical revenue, the Beys went deep into debt, were forced to accept a European financial commission to run their

1881   affairs. France, with the tacit approval of Bismarck and Britain and the envious disapproval of Italy, invaded Tunisia and proclaimed it a Protectorate.

1930's   Tunisian Nationalism began to stir and organised itself into the Destour (Constitution) and Neo-Destour parties. During World War II the

1942–43   Axis occupied Tunisia with Vichy acquiescence, were expelled after heavy fighting by British, American, and Free French forces.

1951   Political reforms demanded by Tunisian Nationalists were rejected by the French Assembly. Guerrilla fighting and political assassina-

1954   tion flared for three years, until Tunisia won independence. The Beys were deposed, Tunisia declared a Republic, and Habib Bourguiba be-

1957   came the first President.